Container Gardening
FOR THE CARIBBEAN AND THE TROPICS

Marilyn H.S. Light

CARIBBEAN

© Copyright text Marilyn Light 1999
© Copyright illustrations Macmillan Education Ltd 1999
© Copyright photographs, except cover photographs, Marilyn Light 1999

All rights reserved. No reproduction, copy or transmission of this publication may be made without written permission.

No paragraph of this publication may be reproduced, copied or transmitted save with written permission or in accordance with the provisions of the Copyright, Designs and Patents Act 1988, or under the terms of any licence permitting limited copying issued by the Copyright Licensing Agency, 90 Tottenham Court Road, London W1P 9HE.

Any person who does any unauthorised act in relation to this publication may be liable to criminal prosecution and civil claims for damages.

First published 1999 by
MACMILLAN EDUCATION LTD
London and Basingstoke
Companies and representatives throughout the world

ISBN 0–333–73143–3

10 9 8 7 6 5 4 3 2 1
08 07 06 05 04 03 02 01 00 99

This book is printed on paper suitable for recycling and made from fully managed and sustained forest sources.

Typeset by EXPO Holdings, Malaysia

Printed in Hong Kong

A catalogue record for this book is available from the British Library.

Photographs by Marilyn Light and Michael MacConaill

Cover illustrations courtesy of *THE GARDEN PICTURE LIBRARY/ Freidrich Strauss* (front) and *Chris Huxley* (back).

Front Cover: *Nerium oleander*
Back Cover: *Tillandsia*

Contents

Acknowledgements		v
Introduction		vii
Understanding Plants in Containers	Choosing containers	1
	Potting medium, soil and soil-less mixes	3
	Planting in a pot or tub	8
	Planting a hanging basket	8
	Creating a water garden	10
	Planting a water garden	12
	Planting a terrarium	12
	Feeding	14
	Watering	15
	Growing conditions	16
	Troubles	17
	Pests and diseases	19
	Moving containers	22
	Ways and means of propagation	24
	Raising plants from seed	28
Decorating with Plants in Containers	Matching containers to plants and situations	31
	Plants for containers – outdoors and indoors	32
	Pots of colour	34
	Tubs of foliage and fruit	36
	Create a patio tree or standard	37
	Sized to fit – dish gardens and terrariums	38
	Fun with herbs	39
	Adventures with bonsai	40
	Water gardens in miniature	43

Plants for Containers Bulbs, corms and tubers 45
Cacti and succulents 49
Ferns 52
Gesneriads 54
Herbaceous plants – annuals
and perennials 56
Orchids 64
Palms and cycads 66
Shrubs and trees 69
Vines and twiners 76
Water plants 77

Appendix I Suggestions for Bonsai-style
Culture 81
Appendix II Suggestions for Terrarium
Planting 82
Appendix III Variegated Foliage Suggestions 83
Appendix IV Useful Resources on the World
Wide Web 84
Appendix V Plant Selection Guide 87
Appendix VI Plant and Seed Sources 92

Glossary 94
Bibliography 97
Index of Plant Names 98
General Index 104

Acknowledgements

The author wishes to thank Michael MacConaill for his photographic assistance especially with the black and white illustrations. His help in formatting the manuscript was also greatly appreciated.

Introduction

Why grow plants in containers? In the first place, pots can be moved: they can be trundled in and out of shelter; displayed only when in peak bloom; or assembled and moved apart according to season, moods, or for special occasions. When in containers, plant roots grow in an environment managed by the gardener. Potting soil that is blended to suit individual specimens means that plants with entirely different needs can be raised in close proximity: those needing acid soils can cohabit with lime lovers. Furthermore, if the soil has been heat-treated before planting is done, soil-borne pests and diseases are controlled. Container culture allows us the ultimate flexibility in gardening. We can as easily bring the glory of permanent flower beds to a patio area and shrubbery to a bonsai-type planting as we can contain the wonder of the forest floor in a glass bottle.

Understanding Plants in Containers

Plants growing in containers can be compared to garden plants established along a dry streambed. Container-grown plants are dependent upon the gardener for the provision of water and adequate light to prosper. With regular care and attention, plants growing in containers will thrive. They are much less vulnerable to the vagaries of weather. Where the plant growing along a streambed is unprotected from a rush of flood water or prolonged inundation, a container-grown plant can be moved out of harm's way if and when the need arises.

Success with container gardening lies in the care and attention of the gardener to detail. Plant selection and matching with an appropriate container, choice of potting medium, watering and application of fertilizer at appropriate intervals will all have an impact on the ultimate success.

Choosing containers

Modern pots are made of plastic or terracotta clay. Impervious, lightweight, plastic pots may be black, green or rusty brown which matches with most foliage types. Plastic pots are furnished with one or more drainage holes in the base. More holes can be made simply by heating a nail and pressing it into the plastic. Water-permeable, heavy clay pots are brick red. Usually, there is one drainage hole in the base. Terracotta pots may be partially or fully glazed, with or without a decorated exterior. Lighter weight plastic pots are especially useful in the home where the chance of wind blowing a plant over is much reduced. Soil in plastic pots dries more slowly than soil in porous clay containers. Cacti and succulent plants are better raised in clay pots where there will be less chance of the compost ever becoming waterlogged. Decorated pots should be carefully compared with the colour of the expected flowers before planting. If the effect could be at all garish or busy, it would perhaps be best to reserve the decorated pot for foliage plants alone.

TABLE 1 Pot capacity in imperial and metric measures according to pot diameter

Diameter (in)	Diameter (cm)	Volume (imperial) (cups)	Volume (metric) (ml)
2	5	0.3	83
3	7.5	1.0	250
4	10	2.0	500
5	12	4.5	1125
6	15	8.0	2000

It is sometimes useful to know the quantity of soil a container will hold, especially when estimating the quantity of fertilizer or pesticide to be applied (Table 1).

Hanging baskets, made of wire, solid plastic, plastic mesh, wood or even pottery, can be purchased or made from existing materials. These are ideal containers for vines, trailing plants and ferns. The larger the basket, the less there will be a problem with drying out. Line baskets with either plastic, coconut 'cloth', or long fibre moss. Punch holes in the plastic to provide drainage. Liners hold fine soil in place yet permit drainage and aeration. Wall baskets or half pots in a variety of materials are popular choices because they lie flat against a support. Outdoors, they are less susceptible to wind damage. Indoors, they save space and are out of the way. Fasten hanging containers securely to their support.

> *Tip!* When attaching a bracket to masonry, use screws of appropriate length with a matching anchor.

The current trend in pots and baskets is towards self-watering devices including raised, perforated bases and water reservoirs. While these devices do work, they may lead to false security with respect to watering. A plant growing in full sun on a hot, windy day can transpire considerable quantities of water. The larger the plant surface area, the more water will be needed. The small reservoir may simply not provide enough for the plant's requirements.

Be a bit unconventional. Every sort of implement is potentially a plant container including the proverbial kitchen sink, bathtub, halved steel drums and even punctured rubber balls. Lined drums can be cut in half lengthwise as tubs for raising tuberoses or Ground Orchids (*Spathoglottis*) or crosswise to hold trees and shrubs. Holes have to be drilled to provide drainage. Wherever the liner has been cut, the steel will be exposed and will eventually rust unless painted. The discarded sink or bathtub is already furnished with a drain. Dig an appropriately sized hole in the ground to partially bury the sink or tub. Use stones as additional drainage to partly fill the hole, place the tub on the stones and fill in the gaps with soil. Only the rim of the sink or tub should rise above soil level. Fill the container with soil and plant whatever you fancy to create a veritable tub of blooms.

Potting medium, soil and soil-less mixes

WHAT IS SOIL?

Soil provides an anchor for roots. It shelters delicate feeding roots from drying wind and burning sun. Soil may at the same time provide air, water and nutrients to roots so that they and the leafy plant can grow.

Many soils are imperfect. They may be too loose and unable to anchor a growing plant sufficiently or they may be too compacted, preventing roots from growing within. Water passes right through loose soil but may not even penetrate heavy earth. An ideal soil mix provides a balance of water and air, perfectly drained yet water retentive. Its chemical characteristics allow for gradual release of nutrients to feeding roots. Most plants grow well in soil that is slightly acidic (pH 6–6.5). Soil acidity may be increased somewhat by adding organic matter or reduced by the addition of horticultural lime.

Garden soil may be a reservoir for nematodes and diseases particularly injurious to plants in containers. Before using raw soil, first heat-treat it or apply pesticide to rid it of nematodes. Treated soil may then be blended with other components to improve its characteristics. Adding sand or grit to heavy soil will improve the texture, making the soil more porous. The addition of well-decomposed compost will improve the water-holding capacity and nutrient status of a mixture.

PREPARING PEST- AND DISEASE-FREE SOIL

To rid garden soil of pests, disease organisms and weed seeds without undue damage to the soil itself, process it in the oven at 82 °C (180 °F). Spread out moist soil on a tray in a layer no deeper than 10 cm (4 in). Use a meat thermometer in the soil to monitor the

FIGURE 1. Soil
(a) From the top, clockwise: vermiculite, sand, soil-less mix, compost, garden soil, and in the centre, perlite.
(b) Assemble components in desired proportion and mix thoroughly.
(c) Test moist soil for porosity by squeezing a handful: the mass should just hold together.
(d) When potting plants, firm the soil then water thoroughly.

temperature. Once the soil temperature reaches 82 °C, process for 30 minutes at that temperature, no higher. Remove the processed soil from the oven and let it cool for 24 hours before using.

> *Tip!* Microwave oven method to heat-treat small quantities of soil. Small amounts of moist soil may be processed in a microwave oven at *HIGH* for 3 minutes. Spread the soil out on a paper plate and process. Allow processed soil to cool before mixing or potting.

SOIL-LESS MIXES

While soil can be blended to near perfection to meet most plant requirements, soil-less mixes are some of the best growing media for small to medium size containers. Not only are these lightweight mixes but they have also been heat-treated to be free of harmful pests and disease organisms. Purchase soil-less mixes ready to use or prepare the equivalent from equal parts of sieved compost, Perlite®, vermiculite (expanded mica) and chopped sedge or sphagnum peat. As these mixtures contain few nutrients, plants growing in them must be fed regularly while in active growth. A small amount of horticultural lime added to the mix will buffer acidity and provide a source of calcium. Once these prepared mixes dry out, they can be difficult to moisten (Figure 1).

A very absorbent copolymer of polyacrylamide can be purchased separately or may be already incorporated in a ready-to-use soil mix. If so, this will be indicated on the package. The product is particularly useful to extend the period required between waterings.

BLENDING SOIL COMPONENTS

Lightly moisten soil components before mixing. Add lime, fertilizer pellets or copolymer chips once soil components have been blended. Wear gloves.

All recipes are given in *parts* of a component. The *part* can be of any convenient size such as a spoonful, a potful, a pailful, etc. Small quantities can be mixed in a pail or on a piece of newspaper. Combine larger amounts in a wheelbarrow or on a large piece of canvas. Be especially careful to disperse additives such as lime or slow release fertilizer pellets evenly through the mix. Use soil soon after it has been mixed (Table 2). Soil left to stand in the rain will tend to separate into components: valuable nutrients will be washed away.

TABLE 2 Selecting potting medium – select the most appropriate potting medium from the table

Type	Texture	Components	Mixture
Shrubs	medium	soil, compost, sand	1a, 1b
Trees	medium	soil, compost, sand	1a, 1b
Palms	medium	soil, compost, sand	1a, 1b, 1c
Bonsai	medium coarse	grit, soil, compost	2
Cactus	porous	grit, compost	3, 9
Succulents	porous	grit, compost	3
Annuals	medium	soil, compost, sand	1a, 1b
Perennials	medium	soil, compost, sand	1a, 1b
Bulbs	medium	soil, sand, compost	1b, 1c
Ferns	water retentive	compost, sand	4
Bromeliads	porous	bark, peat, perlite	4, 5
Orchids	very porous	bark, moss, or shards	4, 5, 6, 7, 8
Baskets	lightweight, porous	soil-less mix, moss lining	9, 10
Water plants	heavy, anchoring	soil, grit	11
Gesneriads	porous yet water retentive	soil, peat, compost	12, 13
Terrariums	layered	soil, compost, sand–gravel	14

1a   2 parts soil, 1 part compost, 1 part sand
1b   2 parts soil, 2 parts compost, 1 part sand (more water retentive)
1c   1 part soil, 1 part well rotted manure, 1 part compost, 1 part sand (for acid-loving plants)
2   2 parts soil, 2 parts compost, 1 part gravelly sand or grit
3   2 parts coarse sand or grit, 1 part compost
4   1 part peat or soil-less mix, $\frac{1}{2}$ part compost, 1 part coarse sand, grit or perlite
5   large pieces of bark or chunks of tree fern
6   New Zealand Sphagnum Moss
7   Bark chips
8   Inert coarse materials, clay pot shards, brick
9   3 parts peat, 1 part vermiculite, 1 part perlite
    50 ml of horticultural lime per 8 litres of final soil mix
10   Long fibre moss
11   2 parts clay loam, 1 part compost, 1 part grit
12   1 part soil, 1 part soil-less mix
13   1 part soil, 1 part peat or compost, 1 part vermiculite
14   1 part soil, 2 parts peat or compost, 1 part coarse sand over a layer of coarse gravel

FIGURE 2. Plants and containers
(a) An unglazed 'Strawberry' pot is partially filled with soil before planting.
(b) Rooted cuttings of *Peperomia* 'Moonset' are separated prior to planting.
(c) A pink, white and green variegated form of *Peperomia macrophylla* is planted in side cups for contrast.
(d) More soil is added after each plant is introduced until, at the very top, a trailing *Peperomia distichia* is set in place. This collection will be drought-tolerant: Bright filtered light will maintain the handsome variegated character

Planting in a pot or tub (Figures 2 and 3)

1. Prepare about one and a half times the quantity of soil or other material needed for a given container and plant type.
2. Remove the plant from the old container. If the roots seem very numerous and tangled, prune them so as to break up the root ball. A powerful jet of water can help to further loosen compacted soil.
3. Choose a container with adequate drainage holes. The capacity should permit additional root growth.
4. Position the roots in the new container such that as soil is added, the original position of the stem(s) with respect to the soil surface will be maintained.
5. Add about half of the soil, tap the container and water well. Be certain that no air pockets remain within the root ball. Add more soil, tapping and pressing firmly after each addition, until the container is almost filled. Water well.
6. Top the soil with small stones, decorative mulch or coarse sand/gravel if desired.

> *Tip!* Double potting, which is placing a potted plant within a decorative jardinière, basket or similar impractical pot, permits us to enjoy the container exterior while providing for the plant within a conventional pot. A saucer should be provided if the decorative item could be damaged by water.

Planting a hanging basket

1. Choose a basket appropriate to the intended use. Small, shallow baskets will hold less soil and require more frequent watering but may be ideal for delicate plants such as Achimenes which succumb in soggy conditions. Large wire mesh baskets will permit planting both into the top surface and also into the sides. If using a mesh basket, first line it with coconut 'cloth' or moss.
2. Partially fill the basket with soil or soil-less mix.
3. Plant several rooted plants/cuttings evenly spaced over the top surface. This could be three or five with the fifth plant positioned in the centre. Water well. Add more soil but leave space between the soil surface and the basket edge.
4. If planting into the sides of a basket, make holes in the moss with your fingers and position plants or rooted cuttings such

FIGURE 3. Corms, rhizomes and tubers
(a) From the upper right, clockwise: Gloriosa Lily tubers, Caladium corms, Tuberose tubers, and an Agapanthus rhizome.
(b) Plant Caladium corms such that the soil just covers the growing points.
(c) Gloriosa Lily tubers require a deep pot to accommodate their length. Add soil just to surround but not to cover the growing points.
(d) Support climbing Gloriosa Lilies with a trellis or pole.

that they face upwards. Tuck in more moistened moss to keep the plants firmly in place. Water well.
5. Hang baskets temporarily in a sheltered area for a few days until growth resumes. Pay careful attention to watering: some baskets will dry out more easily than others. Gradually accustom plants to stronger, preferably all round light.
6. Display the basket where the plants may be admired at eye level.

> *Tip!* Plant three rooted bougainvillea cuttings into a deep 25 cm (10 in) basket. Let the plants grow about 15 cm (6 in) then cut the branches back by two-thirds. After new shoots have grown about 20 cm (8 in) cut them back again, this time to about half their length. Allow for an additional 25 cm (10 in) branch growth then prune this by one-third. The process will produce bushy, densely branched plants ready to produce a wealth of bloom.

Creating a water garden

Water gardens can be established in wooden, plastic or metal tubs, drums, or in poured concrete forms. Tabletop gardens can be created in a glass bowl or within a decorative piece of wood (Figure 4). Larger ponds can be lined with UV-resistant black flexible rubber to seal the surface against water loss and also to protect plants from harmful substances leaching from the construction materials. Liners are safe for both plants and fish. An overlay is not needed for small single containers but will be needed if several tubs are to be linked one above the other to achieve a trickle effect. In-ground or raised ponds can be equipped with a circulation pump and filtration system. The pump flow rate (litres/hour; gal/hour) should allow complete circulation of the pond volume within an hour. An overlay will minimize water loss between containers. It is not necessary to purchase an overly large liner to accommodate all tubs together. Line each container, laying the uppermost liner piece over the liner below and so forth. Allow an additional 60 cm (2 ft) or more to both the length and the width for an overlay if required. An overlay can be disguised with foliage plants or stones.

> *Tip!* Formula for calculating pond liner size
> Length + (2 × Depth) = Length measurement
> Width + (2 × Depth) = Width measurement

FIGURE 4. A small water garden
- **(a)** Very small water gardens can be assembled in a bowl or as seen here, in a hollow, weathered piece of wood. Mount the container for stability then line it with a piece of waterproof plastic.
- **(b)** Disguise the liner edges with pebbles, shells, or even a tiny figurine such as a glass frog.
- **(c)** Plant the garden with appropriate size material, here floating Water Hyacinth and Water Lettuce that have been kept small by repeated root pruning.
- **(d)** Water Lettuce produces miniature offsets which can be removed to keep the garden always in proportion.

Planting a water garden

Lotus and waterlilies grow best if planted in rich soil. When growing several different kinds of plant together in the same pond, use perforated plastic or wooden planting containers to keep the plants separate and easier to maintain. This is not necessary when, for example, a single waterlily or lotus is planted in a tub.

1. Plant lotus tubers horizontally such that the growing point is not covered.
2. Plant waterlilies with the crown just at the soil surface.
3. Use fertilizer tablets (nitrogen, phosphorus and potassium in the following ratios: 10 : 15 : 10 + micronutrients) specially formulated for water plants at a rate of one tablet to 5 litres of soil or according to manufacturer's instructions.
4. Cover the soil with 2.5 to 5 cm (1–2 in) of washed gravel.
5. Grow lotuses with about 10 cm (4 in) of water over the growing point. Waterlilies require a minimum of 15 cm (6 in) of water over the crown.
6. Place other water plants such as papyrus in 2.5 to 7.5 cm (1–3 in) of water. Containers can be raised to the appropriate height on bricks or stones.
7. Floating plants are the easiest to plant: simply lay them on the water.

Planting a terrarium

A glass-enclosed garden requires particular care when deciding what to plant in it as these things, living or not, will all interact as the garden evolves.

1. Place a coarse textured drainage layer in the terrarium before adding soil. This coarse material, consisting of 1 part horticultural charcoal and 3 parts gravel, will act as a reservoir for excess water. Charcoal helps to keep the soil fresh. The drainage layer can be separated from the soil layer by a piece of fibreglass screening if desired.
2. Add moist, porous soil. One-third to one-quarter of the container depth will be made up of soil and drainage materials. The base is typically horizontal but a slanted or landscaped planting surface may also be considered as it will permit a greater variety of micro-environments within the container.
3. Clean the inside of the container using a piece of paper towel (Figure 5).

(a)

(b)

(c)

(d)

FIGURE 5. Preparing dish gardens and terrariums
(a) After assembling a terrarium, clean the glass with a piece of paper towelling.
(b) Handle spiny cacti with folded newspaper or tongs to save both hands and plant from damage.
(c) Position tallest plants towards the centre with smaller specimens to the outside.
(d) Once planting is finished, place stones so as to accent the cacti. Cover soil and fill spaces between plants with gravel or coarse sand as desired.

4. Assemble plants. Remove them from their pots, shaking the roots free of most soil. Trim overly long roots and any damaged or yellowing foliage.
5. Position the plants before actually planting. See how it all fits together. After any necessary adjustments, dig holes in the soil and begin planting. Plant from the centre out or from one side to the other. Once all is planted, firm all in place and water. Water should penetrate to the drainage layer.
6. Keep the terrarium out of bright light and loosely closed for a few days until plants start to establish themselves. Move the terrarium to its permanent position and enjoy it.

Feeding

Choice of fertilizer and application method depends very much upon the plant being grown and how long it is expected to remain in the original container. Most plants benefit from small, regular feedings: infrequent, concentrated application may cause damage. Plants grown primarily for their foliage should be fertilized with a product containing more nitrogen (N) such as 20(N) : 10(P) : 10(K) while plants grown for their flowers should be fertilized with products containing proportionately more phosphorus (P) and potassium (K) as in 10(N) : 15(P) : 15(K). Apply fertilizers as a liquid feed prepared according to manufacturer's instructions or incorporated into the soil at the time of planting. Resin-coated slow-release fertilizer products feed continuously for up to a year. Look for products containing chelated trace minerals. If foliage becomes chlorotic (yellowed), plants can benefit from supplementary feeding of chelated iron. Preferentially use locally available products specifically designed for feeding Citrus and other plants including water plants. Enquire.

Shrubs, trees and palms may remain in the same container for three to five years. In these situations, liquid feeding will adequately supplement what may have been originally incorporated into the soil mix. Regular mulching or top dressing with well-rotted compost will also prove beneficial.

FERTILIZER APPLICATION

Dissolve or dilute fertilizer according to manufacturer's instructions. Apply in recommended quantity only when plants are actively growing. If plants become floppy with elongated shoots, the fertilizer application rate or frequency may be out of balance with the amount of light the plants are receiving. Discontinue fertilizer application and reduce watering frequency, at least temporarily. Try exposing the plant to stronger, indirect light: observe the response. An alternative approach is to change the fertilizer formulation. Observe newly acquired plants and adjust fertilizer application to suit the plant and the growing conditions.

If slow-release fertilizer has already been incorporated into the soil, apply additional fertilizer only after the first year.

Watering

For all kinds of container planting, the key to success is root health. Most container-grown plants dislike soggy soil and will show the grower their distress by dying! To avoid such a catastrophe, ensure that the soil mix is perfectly drained and that there is adequate drainage in the container.

Many plants are sensitive to excess mineral salts. Tap water will contain dissolved mineral salts whereas rainwater or deionized water will not. Salts will gradually accumulate in a container as water evaporates. A white or brownish crust will form on the soil surface: plants may appear distressed. Since water quality varies greatly from region to region, sometimes being very hard or brackish, it is wise to use only water of known quality. While rain will leach excess minerals from container-grown outdoor plants, indoor plants will be more vulnerable to watering from the tap. Watering indoor plants with rainwater or deionized water is therefore highly recommended.

Water containers thoroughly such that water flows out of the drainage openings. Allow the soil to dry on the surface before re-watering. Alternate watering with plain water and fertilizer application. This will minimize salt accumulation.

AUTOMATED WATERING

Automated watering systems are especially useful while travelling or when away at work. A weatherproof, 24-hour timer will coordinate drip and soaker watering in your absence.

Drip watering saves both water and time, providing a low pressure, slow delivery of water to the root zone where the water is needed. An adjustable valve placed in each root ball permits control of the quantity of water (0–20 litres; 0–4 gallons per hour) delivered to any one container or hanging basket. Drip kits include faucet connectors, tubing, mounting clips and valves.

Soaker systems may be used to water tubs, hanging baskets and raised garden beds. Lay an appropriate length of perforated soaker tubing on the soil surface. If the tubing is not hidden by the plant material it can be disguised by mulch. Soaker kits consist of distribution and soaker tubing as well as tube couplings and faucet connector.

GOING AWAY ON VACATION?

Most plants can be left indoors for a week or two with a minimum of attention. Move any plants away from direct sun or where they may be buffeted by wind. Water the plants well but do not fertilize them during the few weeks before departure. Clay pots will be the first to dry out. Wick watering systems can be employed to keep smaller plants evenly moist at the roots. A piece of lantern wick embedded in the soil and thence into a saucer of water is all that is needed. Ask a friend to check indoor plants weekly and to care for those containers that must remain on the patio or in the garden. List the water requirements of each container.

Growing conditions

TEMPERATURE

Cool-growing plants raised in warm climates may be more vulnerable to disease, especially if grown with inadequate light and/or if not carefully watered. Gerbera or Transvaal Daisy grows better at moderate temperatures, 15–22 °C (59–71 °F) in full sun. When raising these plants at higher temperatures, avoid crown rot by planting in deep pots of well-drained soil with the crown just above the firmed soil surface. Top the soil with a generous layer of pebbles or coarse grit.

AIR-CONDITIONING

Warm-growing plants confined to air-conditioned interiors are equally stressed and susceptible to problems, particularly root rot. Position containers away from the appliance outlet.

INDOOR LIGHTING

All green plants require light to survive although some require much less than others. Plants used to decorate homes and offices must be given enough light for their type if they are to remain attractive and healthy. Plants placed towards a white wall will receive much more reflected light than ones set against a darker surface. Plants with low light requirements such as the *Aglaonema*, Reed Palm and Golden Pothos (*Scindapsus*) are less affected by low light provided watering is carefully done.

> *Tip!* Analyse your lighting situation by holding a square piece of cardboard between the light source and about 25 cm (10 in) from a large piece of white paper held where the plant is to be placed. Bright light will give a distinct shadow, filtered light a pale shadow, and low light gives no shadow at all.

Troubles

SIGNS OF TROUBLE

Check plants regularly. Often the first sign of trouble will be wilting, yellowing and/or leaf drop (*exception*: plants entering seasonal dormancy). The most frequent cause of problems is death of the roots. Feeder roots will die if the soil dries out completely. This can happen because of insufficient water or because water cannot penetrate the root mass. Likewise, if plants are over-watered, too frequently watered or if the soil is imperfectly drained, fine roots can rot. Whatever the cause of root death, remedial action must be swift if the plant is to be saved.

CHECK THE SOIL FIRST

If the soil is moist yet the plant appears wilted, do not add even more water. Instead, remove the plant from the container to examine the roots. Trim all dead root material, wilted leaves and stems, then re-pot in fresh moist soil. Place the plant in a shaded spot and mist regularly until growth resumes. Alternatively, try rooting cuttings, trimmed of wilted leaves and very limp tip growth.

If the soil is dry, the plant is wilted but not yet due for re-potting, first try a thorough watering. Observe the plant for several days to see if it perks up. If the plant recovers it means that the roots were still able to absorb water and growth will resume. If the plant does not perk up immediately, set it in a shaded place for several weeks to see if it will recover. Plants can be quite resilient. Keep soil moist. If the main roots have not been damaged, new shoots will soon appear. At this point, remove wilted foliage and dead stems to

FIGURE 6. Container troubles
- (a) Once roots have filled a container, the plant becomes rootbound and must be re-potted.
- (b) A mismatch of container or soil type and inappropriate watering can kill plants. Here, stagnant soil led to the death of roots and eventual demise of the plants.
- (c) Drought- and heat-tolerant Portulaca succumbs to over-watering in poorly drained soil.
- (d) Insufficient light leads plants to produce spindly stems and few flowers.

improve the appearance. Move the plant to a sunny or partly shaded position, according to type.

If the plant is due for re-potting, perhaps the problem is that it is pot-bound. Roots can accumulate such that water penetrates only slightly (Figure 6). Feeder roots can no longer proliferate. Shrubs, small trees and even some herbaceous plants will benefit from the pruning of about one-third of their roots and above-ground growth before re-potting in fresh soil.

RE-POTTING AND ROOT PRUNING

It is true that some plants flower best when pot-bound but eventually even these plants will reach their limit and begin to decline. Re-potting simply into a larger container will only put off the inevitable. Root pruning will rejuvenate a plant, forcing the production of new feeder roots. The steps are simple.

1. Remove the plant from the container.
2. Using an appropriately sized stick and the hose, loosen the soil such that the roots are exposed. Keep wetting the roots occasionally: do not let the roots dry out.
3. Identify the major roots. Cut these roots leaving about two-thirds of their length. Shake or pull away the cut material.
4. Prune the branches up to one-third of their overall length.
5. Re-pot the plant into fresh soil. Be certain that no air pockets remain.
6. Water the plant well. If desired, use a rooting product such as Superthrive® to stimulate root growth.

Pests and diseases (Table 3)

NEMATODES

Nematodes are microscopic worms that burrow into roots. Severely infested roots become unable to absorb water and nutrients. Roots will appear knotted or unevenly swollen. There will be few small roots. Stressed plants are more frequently infested with nematodes. Heavily contaminated potting soil can also lead to infestation. There are nematode-resistant cultivars, chemical nematicides and other possible treatments to rid plants of these pests but the best way to deal with nematodes is to avoid them. Take above-ground cuttings when propagating infested plants. Use only heat-treated soil and keep containers off the ground.

ROOT MEALY BUGS

Hidden from view beneath the soil, these pinkish insects are covered with a fluffy wax that protects them from injury. Mealy bugs feed on roots, piercing a root with a sharp stylet and sucking the juices. Many mealy bugs can severely weaken a plant. Cacti and succulent plants are especially vulnerable but most plants can be infested.

To control an infestation, remove plants from their containers and inspect the roots. If root mealy bugs are found, wash away the soil and insects. Treat the plants with a dip in either insecticidal soap or with an insecticide locally recommended to control the pest. The insects may be resistant to common products. Certain insecticides do not kill the pest directly, acting instead on their reproductive capacity. These can be quite effective in reducing the frequency of treatment. Once treated, plants should be transplanted to fresh heat-treated soil. To avoid new infestations, check the roots of any new plants acquired for the collection.

SPIDER MITES

The first sign of mite infestation will be pale speckled or silvery foliage. Beneath the damaged leaves will be tiny yellow to reddish mites, each less than a millimetre long. Mites can overwhelm heat- and drought-stressed plants. Thin-leaved plants are particularly vulnerable. To avoid mite infestations, keep plants adequately watered and nourished. If infestation does occur, remove infested leaves to a paper bag and dispose of them. If appropriate to the plant type, prune branches and infested leaves to force new growth. Spray with a miticide such as Kelthane® recommended for use with ornamental plants. Insecticidal soaps and paraffinic spray oils may also be useful, especially with indoor plants where insecticide residues are of concern. Ultrafine oils such as Sunspray® are used at a rate of 0.25 per cent by volume. Plant toxicity can occur when spray is used on susceptible plants such as ferns and conifers, or if the plants are already suffering water stress. Toxicity may also be more apparent when these sprays are used in hot, humid conditions. Ultrafine oils provide excellent long-term control of mites and scale insects on plants grown in air-conditioned buildings.

FUNGAL, BACTERIAL AND VIRAL DISEASES

Plants often become infected with disease organisms when damaged or stressed. A pair of secateurs used to prune a diseased

TABLE 3 Diagnosis of and remedies for pests and diseases in

Symptom	Cause	Reason	Remedy
Wilting	too little water	under-watering	water the plant
Wilting	roots dead	under-watering	begin again; take root cuttings
Wilting	roots dead	soil too hot	insulate container; shade container
Wilting	roots dead	over-watering	begin again; take root cuttings
Wilting	roots dead	disease or nematodes	burn diseased plants remove cuttings from nematode-infested plants begin again using heat-treated soil use disease- and nematode-resistant cultivars
Leaf tip burn	too little water	roots damaged	water plant
Leaf tip burn	excess fertilizer	roots damaged	flush with plain water; begin again
Leaf tip burn	pollutants	leaves damaged	review growing conditions and cultivar susceptibility to sprays
Yellowing foliage	dormancy	natural event	allow plant to rest
Yellowing foliage	nutrient deficiency or imbalance	soil pH	check soil pH, apply chelated iron, re-pot
Yellowing and/or speckled foliage	pests (mites)	too hot and/or too dry for plant	shade plant; keep plant cool with frequent misting; apply miticide
Lack of vigour	insufficient nutrients	soil exhausted	apply liquid fertilizer and mulch; re-pot
Lack of vigour	root mealy bugs, disease	organisms competing for nutrients	re-pot; begin again with new seeds or cuttings

plant can then carry disease to the next plant pruned unless steps are taken to rid the tool of the organisms. To avoid disease transmission, clean tools between plants. Burn or otherwise dispose of infected plants and soil. Containers should be cleaned first with hot, soapy water, scrubbed, rinsed, then soaked in a liquid bleach solution (1 part bleach in 20 parts water) and rinsed again, twice. Secateurs, pruning knives, trowels and other tools shared between plants should be similarly treated after each use.

Moving containers

Moving plants in and out of shelter or from one place to another in the home, on the patio or gallery can be time consuming and hazardous to your back. An extra pair of hands will help greatly when pots need to be positioned on boards, rugs or carts prior to the move (Figure 7).

For occasional moves try the following

1. Roll a container up on to a long board laid upon three lengths of steel piping. Roll the board over the pipe sections: as one pipe section is bypassed, simply move that section to the front of the board and continue rolling. Angle the pipes to control direction of movement.
2. Place a container on an old rug or piece of canvas then pull the rug.
3. Place smaller pots, baskets and tubs in a wheelbarrow or cart.

For more frequent moves, try installing castors on an appropriate sized piece of 2 cm ($\frac{3}{4}$ in) marine plywood. Moulding fastened around the perimeter can serve both a decorative and a utilitarian role. Ring bolts can be fastened to the sides of the trolley to allow for rope attachment. Paint or otherwise coat the wood with a water-resistant product. The wood and castors should be of appropriate strength to support the load.

CASTOR SELECTION GUIDE

For use on hard surfaces, choose wheels with rubber.

Load	Castor wheel diameter
45 kg (100 lb)	65 mm (2 $\frac{1}{2}$ in)
34 kg (75 lb)	55 mm (2 $\frac{3}{16}$ in)
18 kg (40 lb)	44 mm (1 $\frac{3}{4}$ in)

FIGURE 7. Moving them about
(a) When constructing a trolley, use castors designed to carry the intended weight.
(b) A simple board and castor assembly together with a detachable rope pull can be used to move heavy containers over flat surfaces.
(c) Choose baskets whose construction and materials match the eventual load.
(d) Plastic growing bags such as this one brimming with cucumber 'Triple Crown' may be hung from firmly anchored metal brackets.

For use on soft surface such as carpets, choose wheels without rubber.

Load	Castor wheel diameter
45 kg (100 lb)	60 mm (2 $\frac{3}{8}$ in)
34 kg (75 lb)	50 mm (2 in)
18 kg (40 lb)	38 mm (1 $\frac{1}{2}$ in)

If a trolley is to be left in place with plants on it, install lockable castors. Simply roll or push a trolley where you want a plant to be, then lock the castors to keep it in place.

A container with sides (a mobile box) may be constructed with two feet and two castors. Install sturdy handles on the footed side for easy lifting.

Ways and means of propagation

Why propagate plants? We propagate plants either to have more of them or to revitalize specimens or to restore plant health. Propagation methods are easy to master. To ensure success, practise first with less valuable plant material. You will gain confidence with practice and experience. With propagation techniques mastered, you will be able to share favourite plants with friends and neighbours, experiment raising plants in a variety of containers and situations, and even attempt to recover a valuable plant from the ravages of root nematode infestation. Some cultivars are protected by patent and may only be propagated with the written permission of the patent owner.

DIVISION

Clustering plants such as asparagus, bromeliads, ferns, orchids and multi-branched cacti are good examples of plants that can be propagated by simple division (Figure 8). When dividing any plant, first examine it to identify natural division points. Try not to divide a plant into many small pieces. More substantial divisions, each having two or three shoots, will be better able to make the transition to autonomy and be quicker to flower as well.

Using a sterilized knife or secateurs, cut through the stem joining the parts to be divided. Transplant each division into potting medium appropriate to the type. Water carefully until growth resumes.

For cacti, succulent plants and corms or tubers, once divisions have been made, allow the cut ends to dry for a minimum of 24 hours before potting up. For water plants: (i) floating plants such

FIGURE 8. Propagation
- **(a)** Divide Cattleya-type orchids into units of three to four pseudobulbs using sterilized secateurs.
- **(b)** Propagate bromeliad clumps by removal of offsets. One offset is under the thumb.
- **(c)** On the left, an unsuccessful Aloe cutting started in heavy, wet soil. In the middle and on the right, two Aloe cuttings successfully rooted in a very porous medium.
- **(d)** From the upper right, clockwise: Boston Fern (propagate by division), Pilea (propagate from rooted cuttings), and Asparagus Fern (propagate by division or from seeds).

as the water hyacinth are simply divided with a sharp knife; (ii) rhizomatous plants such as waterlilies and lotus should be lifted from the pond and washed free of clinging soil to reveal the natural division points. Each division must have at least one growing point. Cut through the rhizome then plant the divisions in individual pots or boxes.

OFFSETS

Bulbous and tuberous plants produce numerous offsets. Offsets should be removed when these plants are less actively growing or are resting. Certain orchids including reed stem *Epidendrum*, *Dendrobium*, *Phalaenopsis* and *Vanda* produce offsets popularly called keikis which can be removed after roots have developed by simply severing the attachment to the parent plant. Water Lettuce produces floating offsets at the end of runners. Viviparous waterlilies propagate not only through the production of seeds but also by plantlets produced in the centre of mature leaves. There is some value in leaving offsets with the parent plant, at least for a while until the offset has developed sufficiently to be raised independent of the parent. Treat any offset as a miniature version of the parent plant. Use the same type of potting medium but a smaller container.

LEAF CUTTINGS

Gesneriads, begonias, and succulents such as *Graptopetalum* can be propagated from detached mature leaves. African Violet leaves, severed from the parent and placed in a shallow pan of damp vermiculite or sand, will first produce roots and then yield a cluster of tiny plants that will quickly grow to be identical to the parent. Similarly, leaves of Rex Begonia, laid on the surface of damp rooting medium and held in place with hairpins, will root, later developing plantlets along major leaf veins. To encourage rooting of begonia leaves, make shallow cuts at the juncture of leaf veins. Dusting cut surfaces with rooting powder before planting may hasten the rooting process.

Leaves of *Graptopetalum*, *Kalanchoe* and many other succulent plants will root readily if simply laid on the surface of damp sand.

Leaves root best in a medium that is both moist and well aerated. Keep containers in a bright location but always out of direct sun. Once plantlets have several leaves and roots, they may be detached from the host leaf and potted separately.

TIP OR SOFTWOOD CUTTINGS

Taking tip cuttings is one of the easiest ways to propagate herbaceous plants such as Pentas and Coleus. Young branch tips of oleander and jasmine may also be rooted using this method. Cuttings root quickly in moist sand, perlite, vermiculite or in a mixture of half sand and half heat-treated soil. Take cuttings with a sharp sterilized knife, making a clean cut about 10 cm (4 in) from the tip: the cutting should have a minimum of two nodes (Figure 9). Carefully remove any large leaves, taking care not to damage the nodes. Rooting will occur mainly at nodes but may also happen between nodes according to the plant type. If desired, dip the cutting in rooting powder prior to placing it in the propagation mixture. Ensure that at least one node is within and one node is above the medium. Keep cuttings lightly shaded and misted. The rooting process will take several days to weeks. Pot up well-rooted cuttings singly or in groups, according to the plant type and desired effect.

SEMI-HARDWOOD CUTTINGS

Stems of some woody plants such as croton and lantana root more easily if the cuttings include partly mature wood located further back along a stem. Take cuttings as described for tip or softwood (above), except that the cutting should have six to eight nodes. Remove the larger leaves especially at the base. Dip the cut surface in rooting powder before planting. Ensure that two nodes are within the medium. Keep cuttings lightly shaded, misted and carefully watered. Roots should develop in several weeks.

HARDWOOD CUTTINGS

Choose branches with developing bark as a source of hardwood cuttings for the propagation of hibiscus, ixora, bougainvillea and similar shrubs or trees. Cut the branches into pieces 20–30 cm (8–12 in) long, each having a minimum of two nodes, remove the leaves, then dip the cutting bases into rooting powder. Plant the cuttings in moist propagation medium with at least one node in the medium and one above. Keep cuttings lightly shaded and misted during the rooting process which can take six to eight weeks. If a cutting is 'taking', the first sign will be the appearance of new shoots but roots sufficient to support shoot development may not yet have formed. Be patient. A gentle tug on the cutting will help determine if rooting has or has not yet happened.

FRANGIPANI

Entire young branches of frangipani may be rooted in very porous and only slightly moist medium. Sever an entire young branch from the parent plant using a sharp, stout knife. Cut at the branching point and leave to dry afterwards until the latex has stopped flowing. Insert the cut end into the rooting mixture, staking if necessary to keep the branch from moving. The cut end should be no more than 5 cm (2 in) into the medium. Rooting should happen within six weeks. Always leave at least one intact branch on the plant being propagated.

AIR LAYERING (MARCOTTING)

When container plants have lost most of their lower leaves, air layering or marcotting is a simple and effective way to establish a new plant while the part to be removed is still attached to the parent. Air layering will not only improve on all-round attractiveness but it will also promote the development of one or more offsets or suckers once the rooted top has been removed. Many shrubs such as croton, oleander, ixora, Queen of Flowers, and herbaceous plants such as dieffenbachia and dracaena are suitable candidates. Palms cannot be air layered.

To prepare an air layer, make a 1 cm ($\frac{1}{2}$ in) deep cut into the stem just above a node where rooting is desired. Wedge the cut surfaces slightly apart with a piece of wood, bamboo or plastic. Generously wrap the stem and cut area with damp moss. Cover the moss with a clear plastic kitchen wrap. Fasten in place with raffia or cord. To keep the moss continually moist without having to unwrap it, insert a short drinking straw. Water may be added to the moss through the straw. Once roots form, they will be visible through the plastic wrap. Sever the stem beneath the roots and plant the top part in an appropriate medium and container.

Raising plants from seed

Seeds may be the only means of obtaining certain plants when rooted plants are prohibited entry because of plant quarantine restrictions. Check locally for any restrictions on seed importation before ordering stock.

The only way to obtain flowering annuals, selected vegetables and herbs is to raise them from seeds. Furthermore, perennial plants raised from seeds, including cacti, succulents and palms, are

(a)

(b)

(c)

(d)

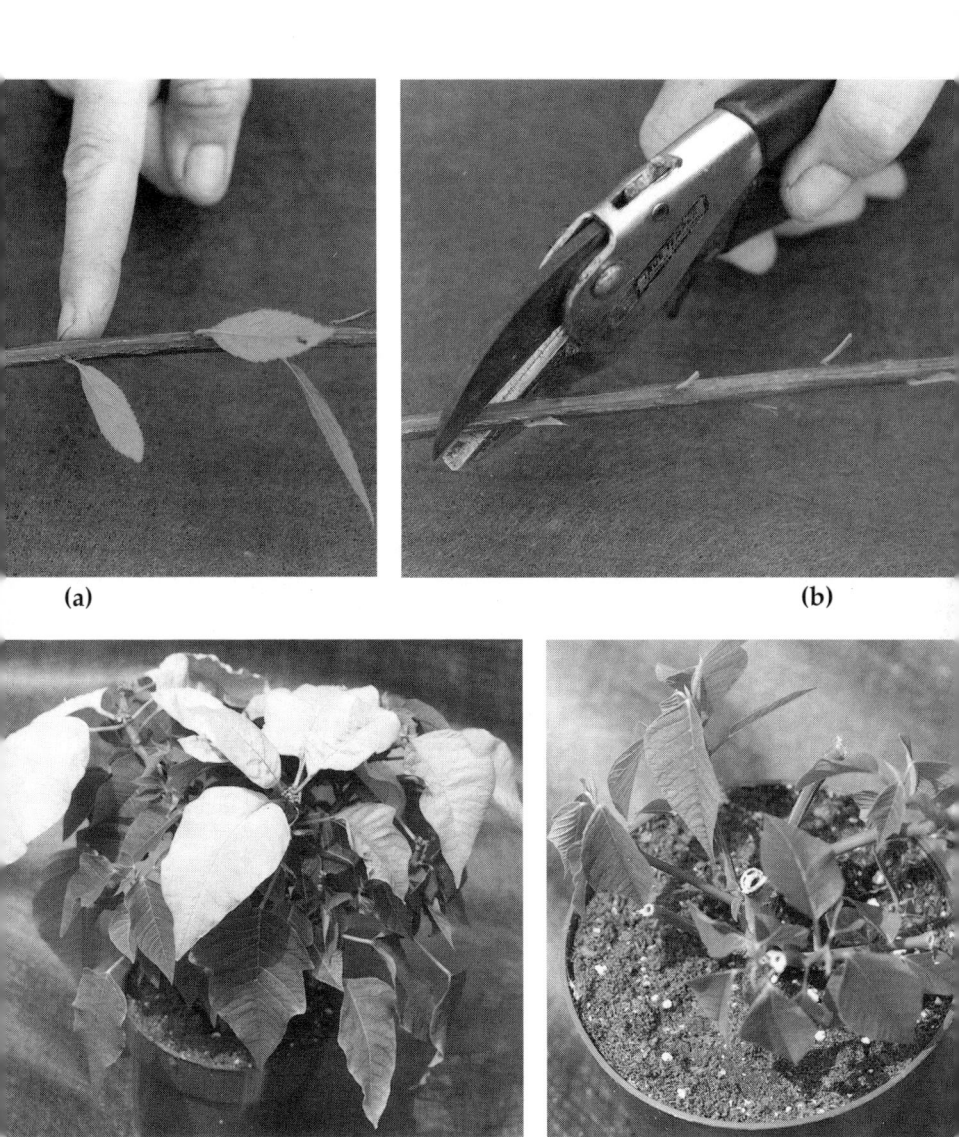

FIGURE 9. Propagation
(a) Along a plant stem are points from which leaves and branches arise. These are the nodes.
(b) When pruning branches or when taking a cutting, sever stems between nodes.
(c) This faded Poinsettia is ready for pruning and for taking cuttings.
(d) Re-pot a pruned Poinsettia into fresh soil, water and fertilize regularly. A second pruning, four months later, will make the plant extra bushy.

far easier to adapt to a container existence than if they are acquired as plants that have had a free root run.

Seed should be freshly harvested and preferably sown as soon as acquired. With a few exceptions, unused seed should be stored in a cool, dry place. Soak large seeds and slow to germinate seeds such as those of palms and certain cacti in diluted liquid bleach for 10 minutes (1 part bleach : 9 parts water) before sowing in heat-treated soil. Pre-treatment will reduce the chance of seed decay before germination.

Cleanliness is crucial to success in raising plants from seeds. Seed trays should be new or first cleaned in hot, soapy water and soaked in bleach solution before rinsing and filling with heat-treated soil. Prepare a germination mix consisting of one part sieved soil, one part sieved compost and one part rinsed sharp sand or crushed perlite, blended and moistened just before using.

Sow seeds according to packet instructions or according to the following general guidelines.

1. Plant fine seeds on the soil surface.
2. Plant larger seeds to a depth of approximately twice their diameter.

Or

3. If light is required for germination, sprinkle seeds on the soil surface or press them into the moist soil without burying them. Spray the seeds with water that has been boiled and cooled. Cover the seed tray with clean glass or clear plastic wrap and keep it in a bright place but out of direct sun. Vent daily. Heat trapped within the tray can quickly lead to death of germinating seeds. (Seeds requiring light to germinate include: coleus, gesneriads, begonia, crossandra, cuphea, gerbera, impatiens, portulaca, petunia, pentas.)

Or

4. If darkness is required for germination, sow seeds according to size as in points 1 and 2 above, then exclude all light until seedlings appear. Black plastic, cloth or several layers of newspaper can be used to ensure complete darkness. It does not hurt to peek occasionally to check on progress. Once the majority of seeds begin germinating, seedlings can be gradually exposed to light and left to develop foliage. (Seeds requiring darkness to germinate include: cleome, euphorbia, gomphrena, verbena.)

Decorating with Plants in Containers

Matching containers to plants and situations

There is an appropriate container for every plant and for every situation. As well as the conventional containers such as plastic pots, even utilitarian objects such as old sinks, tyres and barrels can be adapted to raising plants. Plants may be established in permanent supporting structures such as elevated beds constructed as part of the home or garden or unique containers can be built as needed. Most commonly though, plants will be raised in pots, baskets, pedestal urns or tubs.

While matching upright-growing plants to pots and trailing plants to baskets might be obvious, the question will arise as to which size and style of a container is best suited to each particular plant and situation. Because it is often easier to match a container to a plant rather than the other way around, we should first consider the container at hand including the type of material, dimensions, drainage capacity and outward appearance before deciding what to grow in it. Realize that a few containers are completely inappropriate for growing plants. Metals such as copper are toxic. Exposed metal of cut drums may well corrode leaving a rather unsightly mess. Pots should have drainage holes. Containers without holes can be used but only indoors and with caution when watering. While holes may be drilled quite easily through the base of a porous clay pot, drilling harder ceramics requires skill and a diamond drill bit. Keep glazed, decorative ceramic containers as holders of conventional pots which can be removed for watering and maintenance. Dainty, shallow baskets may be cute but could be disastrous for plants established in them especially if those plants are fast-growing and being raised in full sun. Small containers do not hold sufficient compost and therefore not enough water to provide for quick-growing specimens. Dainty baskets may on the other hand be ideal for petite ferns or gesneriads placed in a humid fernery. Consider the container, the intended growing conditions and the plant requirements before making the match.

Plants for containers – outdoors and indoors

Such is the variety of plants that there is at least one kind for almost every setting. Points to consider are plant size and colour just as one would do with furniture and paintings. Because plants are living things, light, temperature, humidity, wind and salt air (if near the sea) must also be taken into account. Positioning is the key to both visual impact and plant health.

OUTDOORS

The outdoor environment whether it is around the pool, on the patio or at an interval along the garden path, is very much dependent upon the weather. Hot or cool, rainy or dry, plants positioned outdoors have to take what comes. They can be moved of course, and that is a benefit for particularly valuable specimens when bad weather threatens, but one really does not want to be continually moving containers in and out of shelter. A more practical option is to choose plants suited to the prevailing climate. This means selecting masses of sun-loving annuals for the dry season and primarily foliage plants for the rainy season. The practical option suggests using heliconias, bromeliads, calatheas, ferns and gingers in wetter climates, drought-tolerant plants such as cacti, succulents, oleanders, periwinkles and lantanas in drier environments. Gardening near the seashore? Choose salt-tolerant over intolerant specimens. Once a list of suitable plant material has been assembled, it remains to ascertain plant availability and to position newly acquired plants where they best complement the surroundings.

> *Tip!* Air is cooler in the shade. Exploit shady places to your advantage during the hottest times of the year. Especially useful is high shade provided by trees or afternoon shade from a nearby structure.

Tall plants provide shade, form a barrier or a backdrop. Plants with particularly interesting foliage and/or flowers may be used as dramatic focal points in landscape design. Several plants may be grouped for effect but taller accent plants should have minimum competition so that their beauty may be fully appreciated.

Medium-sized plants are fillers. They can also serve to complement or highlight a tall accent plant but should not compete with it. For example, too many variegated plants are confusing to the eye but one striking specimen set against plain leaved kinds is emphasized.
Many smaller plants can be grouped to have impact similar to that of one large accent specimen or they might be positioned singly. Competing backgrounds should be avoided.

> *Tip!* Built-in seating along the sides of a lightly shaded patio is an excellent display area for pots which can be positioned in corners where persons are less likely to sit.

INDOORS

Indoor plants may not have weather to contend with but are equally challenged by the availability of light, perhaps air-conditioning, as well as a complete dependence upon the caregiver for water. Many foliage plants excepting variegated or highly coloured cultivars are quite tolerant of low light but most grow better in good light. Flowering plants require more light to bloom well but many will tolerate low light levels once the blooms are opened. Placing plants near a window may seem to be a solution to light availability but unidirectional, unfiltered sunlight can burn leaves especially when there are no breezes to cool the foliage. Diffuse sunlight using curtains or louvres.

Plants may be used to soften sharp architectural lines of floor, walls and ceiling or to enhance an entry or a decorative pool. Tall plants and hanging baskets should be positioned against walls, in corners or similar locations out of people's way. There should be ample distance between the plant and the viewers when they first enter the room so that the effect can be appreciated. Put some of your best plants on pedestals. Pedestals will set off small plants to advantage and may be grouped at different heights for maximum effect. A collection of small but interesting foliage and flowering plants arranged in a basket is perfect for a guest bedroom.

> *Tip!* Slip decorative cylinders made of grass cloth or coconut matting right over ordinary or ugly pots to freshen your display.

GROUPINGS

Groups of plants having different shaped and coloured foliage can be combined in the same container or pots of different kinds can be grouped for effect. A collection of bougainvilleas assembled on the patio when in full bloom is as spectacular as is an array of dazzling croton cultivars or *Neoregelia* bromeliads in full flush of colour. Unglazed pottery bowls are marvellous as containers for collections of succulent plants such as *Crassula, Echeveria, Graptopetalum*, miniature *Aloe* and *Agave*. Such is the variety of colour, texture and shape that there is no competition for attention. All that is needed is that larger plants are placed to the rear of the display, more diminutive specimens to the fore.

> *Tip!* An open-framed, slat-roofed arbour attached to the home provides shelter from hot sun for people and for plants. Position tubs of sun-loving bougainvilleas just outside and pots of foliage plants inside to highlight the contrast between fiery colour and cooling green.

Pots of colour

THE SINGLE-COLOUR EFFECT

Grouped plants have a natural affinity. A single pot of flowers could be overwhelmed by the sheer scale of furniture and architectural elements but in combination with more of its kind or in the company of other flowering plants, its beauty is reinforced. Try one colour or a combination of complementary shades for a stunning effect. Possible combinations include pink, white, mauve – accent cerise; white, cream, yellow – accent deep orange; white, mauve, pale pink, light blue – accent navy blue; and white, pink, crimson – accent violet blue. For example, grow pots full of drought- and salt-tolerant portulaca 'Sundial' hybrids in shades of yellow, orange, cream and mango. Mix shades at random or arrange pots of separate colours with increasing intensity. A mass of paler colours can be further enhanced by the occasional pot of a brilliant hue. Try combining several similar coloured cultivars together in the same basket, placing this among baskets of each separate colour. Grouping different kinds of plants bearing similarly coloured flowers works well too. Variety and interest arise from the differences in plant shape and height. Pink hibiscus and a cerise bougainvillea can be artfully combined with pots of white and purple-flowered *Cattleya skinneri*. Once the orchids have finished flowering, replace them with pots full of pink periwinkle or tubs of dwarf crape myrtle.

> *Tip!* Containers holding naturally leggy flowering vines can be placed out of sight behind a wall or fence and the tumble of showy branches permitted to drape gracefully over the top for all to see.

A bromeliad 'tree' is a novel way to group these interesting plants without resorting to pots. The 'tree' can be just that, a shapely, branched remnant of a stout tree, or it can be created from mesh wire wrapped around a pole and covered with pieces of bark. If the tree chosen is driftwood, leave it to weather in the rain for a few months so that it is well leached of salt before use as a planting surface. Secure the tree in a suitably sized container, weighting the base with cement or concrete. Before the cement sets, disguise the surface by sprinkling it with pebbles. Alternatively, an indentation can be made in the soft cement to eventually hold a pot of ferns to disguise the base. Allow the cement to set for a day before attaching plants to the tree using wire or monofilament fishing line. Useful bromeliads include *Tillandsia* (medium to high light, humidity), smaller aechmeas such as *Aechmea blumenavil, A. distichantha,* and *A. pineliana* (high light, humidity), or neoregelias (moderate light, high humidity).

THE MULTICOLOUR EFFECT

Gather together a kaleidoscope of colour for a stunning effect. Consider the visual feast presented by a collection of blooming vandas in shades of cherry pink, golden yellow and vibrant blue, highlighted here and there by inclusion of white or ivory shades. Count on a mixture of rich-coloured red, yellow, rose and lavender zinnias to make an equally eye-catching display. Consider the colour of the surface against which the flowers will be displayed. Choose flowers whose colours will not clash or compete with the background. Choose bold yellow, gold, orange and scarlet against a white-washed wall, softer pink, mauve and blue against either weathered wood or darker brickwork. Be willing to try different combinations for effect. Having plants in containers means that choice is always your option.

> *Tip!* Winning basket combinations
>
> Tagetes 'Starfire' + Purple Verbena or Lantana + Zinnia 'Crystal White'
>
> Bidens 'Golden Eye'+ Periwinkle 'Lemon Meringue' + Petunia 'Pink Wave'

Tubs of foliage and fruit

One need not have a spacious garden to raise a variety of favourite fruits and vegetables. Dwarf cultivars exist for a majority of fruit trees and these grow well in containers. Consider citrus grafted on to dwarfing rootstocks such as 'Flying Dragon' and semi-dwarf mangoes including 'Nam Doc Mai' and 'Dwarf Julie'. Bananas such as 'Dwarf Red' are outstanding accent specimens with their red leaf midribs and burgundy trunks. They also yield tasty, reddish fruit.

Plant dwarf fruit trees in wooden barrels cut in half or in similar-sized tubs. Several drainage holes should be cut into the tub base. Bananas and citrus trees are very sensitive to soggy soil. Plant in a mixture of equal parts of compost, sand and heat-treated soil. Incorporate slow-release fertilizer into the mix. After several months, and especially if there has been heavy rain, fertilize bananas with a high potash product such as 16 : 2 : 12 (N : P : K) with added micronutrients. Repeat application at three-month intervals. Fertilize citrus monthly according to manufacturer's instructions with products designed specifically for the crop. Watch the foliage for yellowing (chlorosis) and, if it appears, apply chelated iron. While old pseudostems of bananas should be removed when they decline after fruiting, it is not necessary to re-pot an entire plant at this time. Suckers produced from the base of the pseudostem can be removed once they have roots, leaving one or two to form the next plant. Pot the extra suckers in separate containers. Every five years or so, remove a tree from its container. With bananas, do this after fruit bearing is finished and suckers have begun to form. With woody trees, prune about one-third of the roots and the branches but be careful not to damage the graft union. Re-plant in fresh soil, water well once then hold back on further watering and fertilization until new growth resumes.

Harvest perfect tomatoes, cucumbers, eggplants and peppers without the worry of soil-borne nematodes by raising disease-resistant, compact varieties in containers filled with fertile, heat-treated soil. Use large clay or plastic pots, a minimum of 5–10 L (1–2 gal) size or wooden barrels cut in half. Alternatively, try specially designed, green or brown, cylindrical plastic bags to hold the soil. The bags are pre-cut along one side, ready for the insertion of up to ten growing six-week-old seedlings. These bags may be laid horizontally on the patio or placed vertically against a wall. Vertical bags should be hung in a sunny spot, around the patio, pool or garden. Look for vegetable varieties especially developed for container culture such as the tomato 'Patio' developed by the University of Florida or 'Container Choice' hybrid. Cucumber 'Spacemaster', eggplant 'Slim Jim' and sweet pepper 'Jingle Bells' are remarkably productive in hanging plastic bag containers, much more so than if they were planted directly in the ground!

Tip! Night temperature above 24 °C (75 °F) can inhibit pollen germination in tomatoes: blossoms drop without setting fruit. Plan raising tomatoes during the cooler seasons.

Create a patio tree or standard

For an eye-catching patio accent, train a shrub or tree such as an acalypha, aralia (*Polycias*), bougainvillea, citrus, croton (*Codiaeum*),

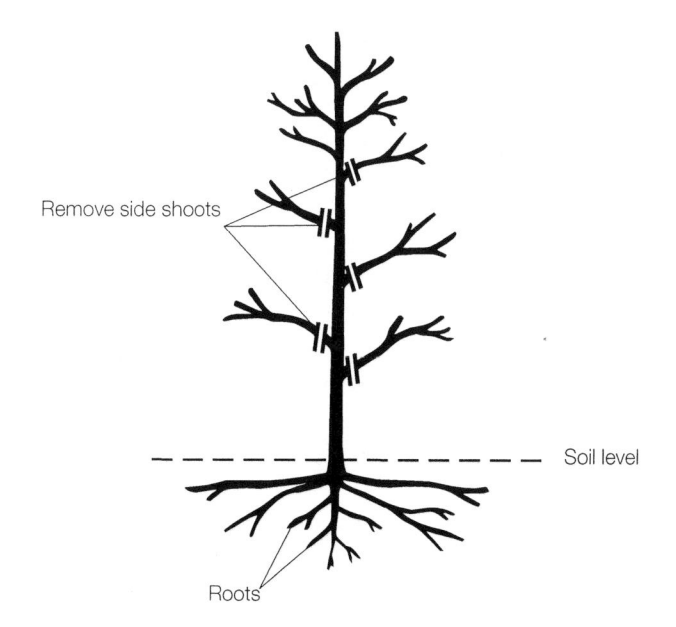

FIGURE 10. To create a patio tree, remove all side shoots until the trunk reaches the desired height.

golden dewdrop (*Duranta*), hibiscus, oleander (*Nerium*), or pomegranate (*Punica*) into a 'standard' shape (Figure 10). Standards or patio trees are plants trained to have a mop of decorative foliage and/or foliage and flowers atop a long straight trunk. Select a vigorous plant or rooted cutting with a straight stem and few side branches. Plant it in an interesting and appropriate-sized container. Stake the plant to keep the stem straight using a stake long enough to accommodate the planned vertical growth. Tie the stem as it grows, to the support using raffia or soft twine. Allow only the leader shoot to grow, removing all side shoots and pinching any new ones as they appear. Provide all-round light to promote even growth. When the trunk reaches the desired height, remove all but the top three to five pairs of leaves from the leader: pinch the growing tip to encourage branching. Pinch these branch tips as needed to encourage even more branching and the eventual formation of the 'standard' head. Remove the stake before putting your handiwork on permanent display. Patio trees will need regular grooming and pinching to maintain the shape.

Sized to fit – dish gardens and terrariums

CREATING VERSATILE DISH GARDENS

The most important step in dish garden assembly is the choice of plants. When combining different kinds in the same container, look for contrast in height, shape, texture and colour. Some plants may be selected for the flowers they will produce and others are chosen more for their foliage. Group together plants of similar growing requirements such as succulents with cacti and ferns with begonias. Before planting, plan your approach. Start with the tallest specimens towards the centre of a bowl or to one side of a rectangular tray. Gradually add specimens, allowing space between them for growth and to avoid injurious rots. Use potting soil according to the kinds of plants being grown. Once all is planted and the soil has been firmed in place, feel free to add pieces of decorative wood, shells, interesting pebbles or figurines.

PLANNING AND ESTABLISHING TERRARIUMS

Terrariums are miniature gardens contained typically in a rounded glass container such as a fish bowl, large brandy snifter or carboy. Within these glass-enclosed worlds, vapour collects, droplets form, and if the containers are closed, rain falls. However fantastic this image appears, closed terrariums are not recommended as they are prone to become mouldy disasters. Planning is the key to success. Balance available space, light and watering to the size and number of plants and the quantity of soil in which they are to grow. Select plants that will grow both in proportion with the container and with each other. Once a container has been selected, assemble appropriately sized tools to work inside. Try fastening a small spoon or fork to a length of bamboo to work within a narrow-necked bottle. To clean glass interiors, use long-handled tongs holding paper towelling. Using a funnel with an appropriate length of tubing attached will not only make the watering chore easier but will also help to avoid messy splashes and time-consuming clean-up.

A terrarium base is typically horizontal but a slanted or landscaped planting surface may also be considered as this will permit a greater variety of micro-environments within the container. For planting material, select from an assortment of naturally miniature specimens such as begonias, fittonias, gesneriads, ferns, orchids and aroids. A piece of a fallen branch already host to tiny bromeliads could be incorporated for added vertical interest. Even the most perfectly planted terrariums will need to be maintained. Depending upon the types of plants, their growth habit and the amount of light received, containers will have to be rotated every few days. Watering frequency will depend very much on the particular situation. When in doubt, under-water, using only rainwater as there is no true drainage. Groom the container and the plants, cleaning the glass inside and outside, removing old leaves and spent blooms. Remove plants if they become too large. With your tender loving care, a glass-enclosed world can bring pleasure for years.

Fun with herbs

Many culinary herbs grow extremely well in the hot, humid tropical climate. These include Spanish thyme also known as Cuban Oregano (*Coleus amboinicus*), Dominican Oregano (*Lippa micromera*), miniature basils (*Ocimum*), Mexican Tarragon (*Tagetes lucida*) and marjoram. Create a wall of kitchen herbs by planting seedlings or rooted cuttings into the hanging, pre-cut plastic growing bags. Work from the bottom up adding additional plants and moist, water-retentive soil until a bag is full. Water well then hang in a temporary place out of direct sun until the seedlings recover and begin to grow. Fragrant herbs will soon cover the plastic and be a joy to behold. Simply water and feed regularly and harvest the herbs as needed for savoury cooking.

A great variety of basil cultivars may be started from seeds. Basils love heat and sunshine. Raise different cultivars in separate pots then assemble the pots together in a tub for effect. Try large-leaved sweet basil, purple-stemmed Thai basil, ruffled leaf 'Green or Purple Ruffles', red-leaved 'Red Rubin', or compact 'Spicy Globe'. Basils are annual plants producing spikes of white or pink lipped, edible flowers.

Cuban Oregano is certainly a herb of choice when preparing fish or pork dishes. The variegated leaf form is not only useful as a culinary herb but is also striking as an accent plant in pedestal urns, tubs or large baskets.

Fragrant rosemary is a Mediterranean herb that can be a challenge to grow in hot, wet climates. Rosemary plants can manage the heat provided the potting mix is slightly acidic and very well drained. Soilless mix or compost blended half and half with coarse sand serves the purpose well. Plants should be raised in full sun. The flexible woody stems and needle-like leaves make this a perfect subject for bonsai-type culture. Furthermore, prunings and extra leaves removed during training may be used in the kitchen (Figure 11).

Adventures with bonsai

Those having small gardens or apartments will be delighted to know that they can have some of their favourite shrubs and trees, albeit smaller versions, growing close at hand. Of the many plants suitable for bonsai-type culture are bougainvillea, *Carissa*, *Ficus*, *Lagerstroemia*, *Malpighia*, pomegranate, rosemary and *Serissa* (Table 4). Each of these plants offers a varied effect and a different challenge. Where bougainvilleas are prized for the splendid ball of bloom that can be had from frequent pinching of new growth, *Carissa*, with a little training and careful pruning, can grow into a stunning cascade shape (Figure 12). Most *Ficus* form aerial roots. Mounting a *Ficus* beside a sculptured rock will encourage hanging roots to bond with the rock to dramatic effect. *Serissa* blooms several times a year but beauty also lies in the impressive gnarled trunk that develops with age. *Serissa* can be unexpectedly deciduous with inconstant culture but this only adds to the horticultural challenge.

In bonsai-type cultivation, plants are miniaturized by containing their sometimes vigorous growth in small containers and by pruning branches and roots. Containers should be of heavy glazed pottery with at least one and preferably three drainage holes. Before planting, these holes will be covered with plastic screening

FIGURE 11. Pruning
(a) This two-year old Rosemary plant, raised from seed, will be branch- and root-pruned to reduce its size.
(b) Prune about two-thirds of the Rosemary branches. Propagate larger semi-hardwood cuttings by rooting in moist sand. Dry trimmed leaves for use in the kitchen.
(c) Separate soil from roots using a plastic or wooden tool. Prune major roots to one-third length, leaving some fine feeding roots intact.
(d) Pot the heavily pruned plant in a new container chosen to highlight the shape. Further top pruning may be done once growth resumes.

TABLE 4 Tropical bonsai candidates

Plant	Effect	Wiring	Branches	Roots	Comments
Bougainvillea	ball	no	pruning	pruning pinching	after blooming
Carissa	upright cascade	yes	pruning	with caution	after blooming
Ficus	ball aerial roots	yes	pruning	pruning	latex will bleed
Lagerstroemia	branching bark colour	yes	pruning: protect bark	pruning	after blooming
Malpighia	weeping	no	pruning weighting	pruning	nematode-sensitive: chlorosis
Rosemary	upright	yes	pruning	pruning	drainage critical
Serissa	gnarled	yes	pruning	pruning	deciduous

to keep the soil in the pot and the pests out. Thread aluminum anchoring wires up through the smaller holes. This wire will be essential to holding a plant in place until it becomes established. Most bonsai plants grow well in a porous mix of earth, compost and gravelly sand.

Vertical containers seem to work better with taller specimens while shallow trays suit more rounded silhouettes. To maintain plant vigour and health, plants are removed from their containers every two to three years when up to one-half of the roots are pruned before re-potting, which is best accomplished when plants are between growth spurts and when just beginning new growth.

Branch pruning is an endless task especially with plants growing more or less year-round. Tropical plants grow quickly. An eye-catching specimen can be produced in just a few years where decades are needed for slower growing temperate species. Consider the form, character and potential of the chosen plant before planning a training routine. Plants with miniature foliage such as *Malpighia coccigera* are especially suited to further miniaturization. Otherwise, dwarf cultivars should be chosen over regular-sized forms for best bonsai effect. It is much easier to train a naturally cascading branch to weep than to force it to grow upright!

Aim for a particular shape, pruning extra limbs and twiggy growth regularly to attain that shape. Training with wire is best accomplished with young growth before it becomes brittle. Starting at the plant base, attach anodized aluminum wire of an appropriate diameter to the anchor wire then wind it firmly up the trunk to the limb to be trained. Start winding part way out on a branch rather than close to the main stem. Be gentle, keeping coils of wire close together along the branch. Wire can be unwound and reset to accommodate increases in a branch diameter. Wire should never be permitted to deform the bark.

Pinch growing tips to encourage side branching for a bushy effect. Remove extra leaves from main trunks and branches but do not remove all the foliage on a stem at once as this can lead to death of that part. Instead, permit a few leaves to remain as these can easily be removed once growth resumes. Where flowering is desired, and especially for those plants that bloom at the tips of new branches, try to prune only after blooming is finished.

Water gardens in miniature

Create a water garden sized to fit into your surroundings. Almost any container will suffice be it a broad glass bowl, a glazed pot, or any cavity that can be lined so that it holds water. Ponds can be

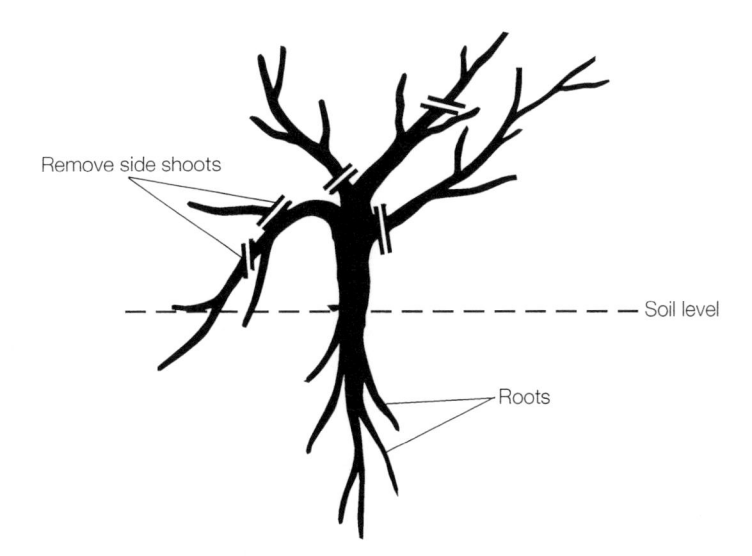

FIGURE 12. Bonsai specimen showing cascade training balanced by an upright secondary branch.

constructed from scratch or be purchased as prefabricated containers in a wide variety of shapes and capacity ready to install. Water plants do need sunlight so placement of whichever container is chosen is critical to success. Ensure that the water garden will receive at least six hours of sunlight a day. All-day dappled sunlight is fine. Where fresh water supply is limited, small gardens may be the easiest to maintain. Even quite vigorous plants such as water hyacinth will exhibit restricted growth in smaller containers.

Plants for Containers

Bulbs, corms and tubers

Plants with bulbs, corms, tubers and rhizomes are some of the most flexible subjects for the avid gardener. Many of these gems may be planted with an eye to the calendar, and with the expectation of flowers and/or decorative foliage within a set period of time. Bulbs, corms and tubers are removed from containers between growing seasons when they must be stored dry or else the parts may begin to sprout prematurely.

AMAZON LILY

Deliciously fragrant, the Amazon or Eucharis Lily (*Eucharis grandiflora*) blooms best when grown confined to a pot. Clusters of about five pure white flowers are borne on sturdy, 50 cm (20 in) stalks above handsome dark-green foliage, two to three times a year. Bulbs should be planted six to a 25 cm (10 in) diameter clay pot, in rich well-drained soil, with just the tip of the bulbs showing. The plants should be lightly shaded. Keep the soil very moist up to blooming, fertilizing heavily to promote flower production. Plant in March to May for flowers several months later. After blooming, allow the plants to dry out somewhat for several months. Heavy watering and feeding will force plants back into active growth and bloom. Propagate by division and from seed.

CALADIUM

Caladiums are widely admired for their brilliantly coloured and patterned foliage. They grow best in semi-shade and so make ideal plants for decorating indoors. Fancy-leaved types have broad, arrow-shaped leaves. Popular cultivars include 'Florida Fantasy' (white with red veins), 'Candidum' (white with green veins), and 'Red Flash' (spotted dark red with green leaf margin). This last cultivar has good sun tolerance and could be used on a patio where plants would be exposed to a few hours of direct sun daily. Strap-leaved cultivars have elongated leaves. Varieties 'Pink Gem' and 'Red Frill' are especially recommended for use in hanging baskets. Plant tubers in well-drained soil. To encourage more foliage, first remove the central bud which is likely to produce a less showy inflorescence and only a few leaves. Cover the tubers with only a little soil. Keep the soil slightly damp until roots become established and leaves begin to unfurl. Thereafter, keep soil moist and fertilize every two weeks. After several months, when older foliage becomes pale and tattered, suspend fertilizer applications and decrease watering frequency to allow tubers to mature and become dormant. Plants may be divided while dormant and then re-potted.

CANNA

Cannas are handsome plants, variegated cultivars being particularly stunning in or out of flower. Grow cannas in movable containers ready to position as an accent or screening plants on the patio or terrace. Plant the stout rhizome, growing point up, in well-drained soil enriched with compost and manure. Cannas are heavy feeders. Water and feed weekly while the plants are actively growing. Raise cannas in full sun. Tall cultivars such as the boldly striped Canna 'Bengal Tiger' can attain 2 m (6 ft) and are best suited for use in very large tubs. More miniature types, such as the All America Award Winner 'Tropical Rose' which grows less than 1 m (3 ft) tall, and can be raised to blooming size from seed in just 90 days, are highly recommended for mass planting in large pots and tubs. Propagate selected plants by division. The Canna Leafroller caterpillar and Canna Rust can severely damage susceptible plants so be prepared to act if these problems arise.

CRINUM

Crinums are medium to large stately plants with leaves up to 3 m (10 ft) long and stout stalks of white to deep pink, fragrant, spidery flowers. Plant bulbs in tubs filled with well-drained sandy soil with the neck of the bulb above the soil surface. As plants may be left to form large clumps, allow sufficient space for the plant to grow and multiply. Mulch annually with coarse compost, cocoa or peanut hulls, bagasse or wood chips. Grow in full sun to light shade. Water and fertilize regularly. Propagate by division and by seed.

ELEPHANT EARS

This group of impressive plants is related to the edible aroids such as tannia. The ornamental Elephant Ears have rhizomes or tubers and large, broad, arrow-shaped leaves in a variety of shades and markings. Some such as the giant green-leaved *Xanthosoma saggitifolia* grow to over 3 m (10 ft) tall while others such as *Colocasia antiquorum illustris* are smaller, just about reaching 1 m (3 ft) in height. The foliage of this latter species has a rich, dark, velvety surface. *Alocasia cuprea* grows to approximately 75 cm (30 in) with shield-like, quilted leaves about 45 cm (18 in) long. The leaf veins are at first deep carmine against a silvery ground. As the leaves mature, the veins and most of the surface become deep bluish green with silvery highlights. Given that the leaf undersurface is deep purple, a well-grown plant can make quite a show. Elephant Ears thrive in rich soil, needing copious quantities of water and high humidity to grow well and to maintain a fresh appearance. They may be grown in full sun or semi-shade according to the type. Plant tubers about 10 cm (4 in) deep in pots half-filled with small stones or broken crock and topped with a coarse mixture of sand, compost, well-rotted manure and soil. During dry weather, stand pots in water. Containers of Elephant Ears may also be placed in shallow areas around a garden pool, the pots disguised by rocks or bricks. Fertilize actively growing plants weekly. Propagate by division.

LILY OF THE NILE

Lily of the Nile or *Agapanthus* is a wind- and salt-tolerant plant having both splendid strap-like foliage and stately clusters of blue or white blooms borne on strong stems. Miniatures such as 'Peter Pan' and 'Rancho' are especially useful for container planting. Plants are evergreen, blooming more freely when crowded and so should not be divided too frequently. The growing tip should be planted just below the soil surface. Propagate by division and from seed. This plant may be short-lived in the hot lowlands: it performs better at higher altitudes.

NARCISSUS

A longtime favourite of northern indoor gardeners, Paperwhite Narcissus (*Narcissus tazetta*) can also be grown in tropical homes and gardens. Unlike other narcissi and daffodils, these bulbs do not require chilling to bloom. Clusters of very fragrant white flowers are carried among slender green leaves. The largest bulbs will produce the most flowers, often several stems per bulb. Plant groups of bulbs about 10 cm (4 in) deep in pots of sandy soil. Water well. Staking may be needed to support flower stems. If staking is desired, place the stakes now. Once roots are growing and until the foliage has matured, fertilize weekly. Grow in semi-shade to full sun. Once blooming is over, place the pots in a sunny, sheltered spot protected from rain, allowing the new bulbs to mature and become dormant. Remove dormant bulbs from soil and store in a dry place for several months before re-planting. Propagate by offsets.

SPIDER LILY

The fragrant, white, spidery blooms of *Hymenocallis* can be produced virtually year-round. Choose a larger tub to accommodate several years' growth and accumulating offsets. Fill with a well-drained blend of soil, sand and compost mixed with a generous portion of well-rotted manure. Plant the large bulbs with their tops about 10 cm (4 in) beneath the soil surface. Water regularly such that the soil never completely dries out. Once established, spider lilies need not be divided for four years. Propagate by division.

TUBEROSE

Marvellously fragrant tuberoses are popular patio plants that will perform equally well in full sun or light shade. The most popular cultivar is 'Double Pearl', a long-stemmed beauty having clusters of double, waxy, creamy-white blooms above grassy foliage. Quite susceptible to nematode attack, these plants are more reliable when raised in containers. Plant the tubers with the pointed green tip uppermost and just above the soil, 10–15 cm (4–6 in) apart in tubs of rich sandy soil. Keep the soil moist. Feed weekly up to the time of flowering. Tuberoses begin blooming about three to four months after planting. Flowers individually last several days but buds open successively over several weeks. Plant successively to have a continuous supply of flowers and fragrance. When blooming has ended and foliage dies back, withhold water allowing the tubers to become dormant. Lift and store the tubers in a dry place for several months before re-planting. A few tubers will quickly multiply by offsets which should be separated from the old tubers before planting.

ZEPHYR LILY

Whether the white, yellow or pink kinds are chosen, these delightful flowering plants will please the grower with copious bloom, often several times a year. As the name suggests, zephyr lilies can arise as quickly as the wind. Heavy watering of dormant bulbs will spur blooming. Plant the small bulbs about 7.5 cm (3 in) deep in clay pots filled with rich, sandy loam. Watering will initiate the first flush of growth and flowers after which the foliage will yellow and become unsightly. There is no need to remove the bulbs from the pot. Instead, remove the pots to a place sheltered from rain. Permit the bulbs to

PLATE 1
1.1 Canna 'Bengal Tiger' is a magnificent accent plant even when not in flower. Photo by M. MacConaill.
1.2 Variegated plants such as Dieffenbachias look their best when displayed against contrasting backdrops. Photo by M. Light.
1.3 During the *Neoregelia* bromeliad flowering period, leaf rosettes flush delicious shades of fuschia and scarlet. Photo by M. Light.
1.4 Create stunning hanging baskets with annuals such as golden-flowered Bidens and multiflora Petunias. Photo by M. MacConaill.

2.1

2.3

2.4

PLATE 2
2.1 Tub-grown Citrus trees respond to quarterly fertilizer application and mulching. Photo by M. Light.
2.2 Cool a hot veranda with potted plants. Photo by M. Light.
2.3 Ornamental banana (*Musa velutina*). Photo by M. Light.
2.4 Star Fruit. When selecting fruit trees to grow in containers, choose cultivars according to local conditions. Photo by M. Light.

2.2

PLATE 3
- **3.1** The plastic growing bag is all but hidden by the miniature Basil it contains. Photo by M. MacConaill.
- **3.2** Pots may be mingled with established plantings. Here, a handsome Coleus nestles among Canariensis bushes (*Galphimia gracilis*). Photo by M. Light.
- **3.3** The variegated form of Spanish Thyme is both a handsome specimen and a tasty kitchen herb. Photo by M. Light.
- **3.4** Impatiens 'Mini-Hawaiian' is picture perfect in a pot or basket. Photo by M. Light.

PLATE 4
- **4.1** Episcia 'Acajou' is never without flowers. Photo by M. MacConaill.
- **4.2** Shown here growing in a small container, *Streptocarpella saxorum* is also recommended for baskets. Photo by M. Light.
- **4.3** Cascading stems of *Columnea microphylla* are stunning in or out of bloom. Photo by M. Light.
- **4.4** Strong, upright stems of Angel Wing Begonias add vertical interest to a collection. Flowers are an added bonus. Photo by M. Light.

5.2

5.1

5.3

5.4

PLATE 5
5.1 *Brugsmansia* 'Jamaica Yellow'. Photo by M. MacConaill.
5.2 Suspend heavy plants such as this magnificent Staghorn Fern from sturdy branches. Photo by M. Light.
5.3 Breadfruit Ferns thrive in moss-lined wire baskets hung in full sun. Photo by M. Light.
5.4 *Zinnia angustifolia* 'Crystal White'. Photo by M. MacConaill.

6.1

6.2

6.3

6.4

PLATE 6
- **6.1** Crown-of-Thorns 'American Beauty'. Photo by M. Light.
- **6.2** Many succulent plants such as this *Crassula* tolerate drought and salt air. Photo by M. MacConaill.
- **6.3** Epiphytic *Rhipsalis* cactus performs well in a hanging basket. Photo by M. Light.
- **6.4** *Parodia auriespina*. Photo by M. MacConaill.

PLATE 7

7.1 Florida native orchid, *Encyclia tampensis*, has been mounted first on individual plaques then grouped together on a post for mass effect. Photo by M. Light.

7.2 Phalaenopsis Queen Stripes and similar cultivars make splendid flowering specimens. Photo by M. MacConaill.

7.3 *Cattleya skinneri* is raised in a wire basket with pottery shards. Photo by M. Light.

7.4 Cycad *Encephalartos munchii* has substantial cones. Photo by M. Light.

PLATE 8
- **8.1** Protect Dracaenas from damaging winds. Watch for leaf tip burn as a sign of under-watering. Photo by M. Light.
- **8.2** The Desert Rose will prosper in full sun if left undisturbed. Photo by M. Light.
- **8.3** Frequent pruning of the Bird Catcher Tree encourages the production of new colourful shoots. Photo by M. MacConaill.
- **8.4** Mexican Heather (*Cuphea hyssopifolia*). Photo by M. Light.

9.1

9.2

9.3

9.4

PLATE 9
- 9.1 Trailing Lantana is a good choice for tubs and large baskets. Photo by M. Light.
- 9.2 Dwarf Pomegranate is an interesting bonsai subject. Photo by M. Light.
- 9.3 A white-flowered Crinum. Photo by M. Light.
- 9.4 Amaryllis (*Hippeastrum*) hybrids like 'Pamela' perform well in the tropics. Photo by M. Light.

PLATE 10
- **10.1** Miniature Waterlily 'Helvola'. Photo by M. MacConaill.
- **10.2** Dwarf Lotus 'Momo Botan'. Photo by M. MacConaill.
- **10.3** White Water Snowflake. Photo by M. MacConaill.
- **10.4** Water Hyacinth. Photo by M. MacConaill.

11.1

11.2

11.3

11.4

PLATE 11
- **11.1** Mount clustering epiphytic *Tillandsia* bromeliads and suspend them on wires of varying lengths for effect. Photo by M. Light.
- **11.2** Bromeliads like *Billbergia* may be displayed in baskets but a darker container in this instance might have been a better choice. Photo by M. Light.
- **11.3** Train branches to assume the desired position by using soft aluminum bonsai wire. Photo by M. MacConaill.
- **11.4** Automatic watering tubes are disguised as part of the basket support. Photo by M. MacConaill.

rest for six to eight weeks then move the pots back to the patio, resume watering and await the flowers. If seeds are produced, these may be sown to increase your collection or to share with friends.

MORE CHOICES

- Canna 'Nirvana', 'Bangkok Yellow', 'King of Siam': tall plants, striped and/or mottled foliage; yellow/orange blooms.
- Canna 'Lucifer': dwarf plant with crimson flowers.

Cacti and succulents

Cactus and succulent plants must be raised in perfectly drained soil. Soggy soil coupled with warmth and high humidity can spell disaster for this interesting group of drought-tolerant plants. Some kinds are much more vulnerable to rot than others, especially those plants that cluster with age. Protect vulnerable above-ground stems from decay by nestling a generous layer of pebbles or coarse grit around the plants. Using a funnel, place some of the grit between clustered stems. A sharp tap will settle the grit in place. To achieve perfect soil drainage, ensure that the soil mix contains a generous quantity of grit such as tile chips, chicken grit, canary gravel or washed coarse sand. The other soil component should be well decomposed, sieved compost. It is a mistake to grow cacti and succulents in impoverished soil. They will grow but will never attain the vigour of specimens grown in richer mixtures.

Cacti

ASTROPHYTUM

Cacti offer a splendid variety of shapes and forms. The white, pebble-textured, spineless 'Bishop's Cap' is no exception. Extremely easy to grow in a container, this cactus can eventually attain great size. A mature plant will further delight the grower with an annual display of lemon-yellow flowers borne on top. To maintain the pristine beauty of the stem, surround the neck with coarse grit or gravel. Water with care. Keep plants sheltered during the rainy season.

ESPOSTOA

The so-called 'Old Man of the Andes' is a marvellous example of plant adaptation to heat and to cold. These columnar cacti are covered by a thick, soft coat of insulating hair. A simple comb may be used to rid the hair of dust and webs. Young plants, easily raised from seeds, are more showy than older specimens. Use young plants in dish gardens, alone or in combination with cacti of contrasting shape and texture. Water with care to keep plants growing slowly.

MAMMILLARIA

Compact, sometimes clustering, these popular plants are easy to grow or raise from seeds. This is the least expensive way to gain a wide variety of plants. When planning a cactus dish garden, choose mammillarias of different shape, flower colour and spination. Contrast simple stems with densely clustered types. Ensure that the plants chosen are not tap-rooted types as these may be difficult to accommodate in shallow planters.

Shallow-rooted types
Mammillaria compressa has a chalky green body with long white spines interspersed with tufts of white hair. Dark spines bristle from the surface of *M. elegans*. Free-flowering *M. erythrosperma* has star-like radial and central hooked spines. All of these species are ideally suited to shallow dish gardens.

Tap-rooted types
Mammillaria uncinata and *M. zuccariniana* require deep containers to accommodate their carrot-like roots. Their spines are short, stout and curved. They can grow very quickly with generous watering and feeding.

MELOCACTUS

This cactus is native to coastal areas of the West Indies and neighbouring Central and South America, and is referred to as the 'Turk's Cap' because of the unusual hat-like flowering structure. Melocacti are shallow rooted, the roots spreading out from the plant in all directions making them vulnerable to damage during transplanting. Plant Melocacti in wide containers. Once the pots are two-thirds full with gritty soil, add a generous layer of coarse sand to protect the plant neck. Grow Melocacti in full sun.

PARODIA

Parodias are very easy to grow and bloom once they have been raised past the seedling stage. After three or four years, species such as *P. aureispina* and *P. sanguiniflora* produce stunning flowers in yellow or flame red which open with the sun over several days.

Plants will cluster with age. These very spiny plants should be handled carefully with tongs, to protect both the hands and the spines. Grow in filtered sunlight.

RHIPSALIS

Rhipsalis are epiphytic cacti that can be found growing in trees in the wild. They are ideal subjects for basket culture, being mostly pendant, curiously shaped and free flowering. Branched stems are variously cylindrical to flattened, garnished with tufts of hair-like spines. Plant rhipsalis in moss-lined baskets filled with compost and a little sand. Water year-round. Hang the baskets in bright but filtered light. Raise these cacti from seed or from rooted cuttings.

Succulents

ALOE

Dwarf and clustering Aloes are worth while considering for a dish garden. Low-growing species form elegant and variously coloured rosettes, topped on occasion with taller flower stalks having yellow to red tubular blooms.

Among those to choose are *Aloe variegata*, the 'Partridge-breasted Aloe', so named because of the dark foliage lightly marked grey green. This species will form a group but offsets can appear some distance from the parent plant. Clustering *A. aristata* has dark-bluish-green leaves covered with fine white projections and edged with soft white 'teeth'. Aloes should be grown in as much light as can be given safely without burning the foliage.

CRASSULA

Within this large group of succulent plants, there are kinds with upright growth habit suited to pot culture and trailing types better suited to baskets. Crassulas should be planted in well-drained sandy soil, grown in full sun to light shade and protected from prolonged rain.

EUPHORBIA

Popular 'Crown-of-Thorns', *Euphorbia milii*, is both compact and free-flowering. This thorny species is best grown by itself in large pots or urns in full sun. Spherical, delicately marked, slow-growing *E. obesa* is best raised in a deep pot. Provide bright filtered sunlight and protection from rains. Both of these Euphorbias grow best in gritty soil mixed with compost. Surround plant necks with additional grit. Water slow-growing species with care. Euphorbias may be raised from seeds or from rooted cuttings. Seeds may take several months to germinate. Keep evenly moist and be patient.

Ferns

Simply mentioning the word 'fern' brings to mind images of refreshing green foliage. Fern greenery contrasts with and highlights hot flower colours. It also provides a cooling refuge for the viewer's eye. Ferns can be grown in pots, baskets, or mounted on plaques of wood or bark. Variously shaped leaves ranging from the simple strap-like fronds of the Bird's Nest Fern, through the lobed leaves of the Breadfruit and Staghorn Ferns and the finely divided segments of the Rabbit's-Foot Fern, can be used for effect, in groups of the same or different cultivars. Massive Staghorn Ferns are best appreciated singly as accent plants, suspended from a sturdy tree limb or hung against a wall in bright, filtered sunlight. Raise the elegant yet massive Bird's Nest Ferns in large pots on a veranda or in a sheltered fernery to protect them from damaging winds. Resilient Breadfruit Ferns and coarser varieties of Boston Ferns are splendid basket subjects for use on an open veranda. Raise more delicate specimens such as the Maidenhair Fern in a humid, shaded fernery. Soil for all but mounted specimens should be porous yet water retentive. All ferns are especially sensitive to pesticides.

BIRD'S NEST FERN *(Asplenium)*
This stunning fern forms a cup or 'nest' of long, glossy, lime-green leaves. New fronds arise from the centre, continually refreshing the display. Raise in bright filtered light in a fernery. Water with rainwater to avoid spots on the foliage. Propagate from spores produced on the undersurface of fertile leaves.

BOSTON FERNS *(Nephrolepis)*
As if geometrically arranged, parallel rows of leaflets enhance the effect of the long, drooping fronds of *Nephrolepis cordifolia*. This tuberous fern is a perfect choice for basket culture in full sun to partial shade. Cultivars include 'Buttons' (leaflets reduced to rounded buttons), 'Tesselata' (each leaf tipped with a tassel); propagate by tubers and by division.

BREADFRUIT FERN *(Polypodium)*
Shiny, dark-green, coarsely divided foliage makes this a popular fern for baskets, pots and tubs in sun or partial shade. Propagate by

placing divisions of the long creeping stem on the soil surface of a new basket. Anchor pieces with bent wire until rooted.

MAIDENHAIR FERN *(Adiantum)*
Delicate Maidenhair Fern foliage is scintillating, composed as it is of numerous wedge-shaped leaflets and wiry black stems. Grow plants in a very humid, semi-shaded place, in individual pots or in baskets. Arrange groups of different cultivars for effect. Overturned clay pots make modest but effective pedestals for containers of varying height. Propagate by spores and by division.

RABBIT'S-FOOT FERN *(Davallia)*
Create a ball of lacy, leathery foliage and curious, furry growing points using the Rabbit's-Foot Fern. Prepare a moss-filled wire basket. Attach pieces of fern rhizome over the top and sides of the basket. Pieces can simply be attached with lengths of bent wire. Hang the basket temporarily in a semi-shaded place, keeping the plants moist and misted until the pieces have become rooted. Suspend the basket permanently where there is light overhead shade.

STAGHORN FERNS *(Platycerium)*
Massive, epiphytic Staghorn Ferns have specialized disc-like leaves which hold plants fast to their support and arching fronds beneath which are brown felted areas where spores are produced. Some of these ferns, such as *P. bifurcatum*, produce offsets which can be removed and raised separately. Staghorn Ferns are best raised on large pieces of bark or wood where they have sufficient space to grow to maturity. Suspend the ferns from substantial tree limbs or from strong, overhead beams of a veranda or fernery. Use sturdy hangers as these plants can be quite heavy when fully grown. Spray plants periodically with a very dilute solution of liquid fertilizer. Propagate from spores or by offsets.

MORE CHOICES

- Australian Tree Fern (*Alsophila australis* or *Sphaeropteris cooperi*): pots and tubs; grow in shade protected from drying winds and salt air; propagate from spores.
- Mother Fern (*Asplenium bulbiferum*): pots and baskets; high humidity; semi-shade; propagate from spores and offsets produced beneath the leaves.

Gesneriads

Gesneriads are a large family of interesting flowering plants having showy blooms. Many kinds have rhizomes or tubers to withstand inappropriate growing conditions while others have long trailing stems or creeping rhizomes. Certain gesneriads produce offsets while others root easily from leaves severed from a parent plant: new plantlets are produced. Many gesneriads can be raised in a bright indoor location where they respond to excellent care. Choice of container depends much upon the growth habit. Trailing specimens belong in baskets, more compact cultivars in pots. Wick watering of potted plants reduces the likelihood of water spots on foliage. To establish a wick system, simply place a piece of lamp wick within and without the pot via the drainage opening. Place the pot in a saucer filled with water and the wick will transport liquid into the pot. Dilute fertilizer can also be applied via the saucer and wick. Groom hairy leaves using a soft brush. It is so easy to propagate these plants that with a few exceptions, this should be done on an annual basis to keep specimens at their best.

ACHIMENES

Achimenes are equally at home near a window in a bright living room or in a lightly shaded balcony planter. There is a wide range of cultivars from species such as red-flowered *A. erecta* and yellow *A. antirrhina*, to large-flowered hybrids such as the trailing 'Cascade Violet Night', bushy 'Paul Arnold', tetraploid blue-flowered 'Tetra Blauer Planet', double-flowered 'White Rose' and hanging basket favourite, 'Purple King'. Achimenes are quite easy to grow provided one respects their annual need for a rest. Withhold water after the blooming is finished. Plants entering a resting period produce scaly rhizomes just below the soil surface. Lift and store these rhizomes together with some dry soil or moss in a paper bag for several months before re-planting. To start new growth, plant the rhizomes in a container filled with moisture-retentive but porous soil mix. Plant six to ten rhizomes of trailing cultivars, 2.5 cm (1 in) apart in a 25 cm (10 in) wide basket. Plant erect, bushy types in pots or in window boxes. Plants can tolerate early morning or late afternoon sunlight, otherwise provide light shade. Feed weekly from the time the plants commence growth until the flowering ceases. Propagate from seed and rhizomes.

AFRICAN VIOLETS (*Saintpaulia*)

Among the most desirable of gesneriads and the most elusive to gardeners in the hot, humid tropics, are the African Violets. Many cultivars simply do not perform well under continuous high temperature. Some, especially those having ruffled foliage, will become plain leaved in the heat. If success is to be achieved it will be with plain leaf, single, dark blue or purple-flowered cultivars. While these are the most reliable, it is still worth while to try something new such as raising new cultivars from seed. Available are trailing types and even those producing variegated foliage. Raise African Violets in light, porous soil such as soil-less mix blended with some compost and sand. Grow out of direct sunlight. Wick water to avoid spotting the foliage with water. Fertilize weekly with a product recommended for flowering houseplants.

EPISCIA

Episcias, valued equally for their foliage and flowers, thrive in hot, humid, shady conditions, in baskets or shallow pots. Episcia 'Pink Acajou' is one of the loveliest with foliage in shades of pink, silvery green and purple. Beautiful as a foliage plant alone is Episcia 'Silver Skies' with cascades of dainty, silvery, pointed leaves. Brick-red blooms are an added bonus. 'Tropical Topaz' may have fewer flowers but these are yellow, a rarity in episcias. Foliage is lime green. Grow episcias in rich moisture-retentive soil indoors in indirect sunlight or outdoors in a fernery or shaded patio, Propagate by cuttings and offsets.

Once included in the genus *Episcia* are *Alsobia dianthiflora*, *A. punctata* and their hybrid 'Cygnet'. Their attractiveness lies with the long cascading stems, punctuated by rosettes of dark-green pubescent leaves and large white flowers. These make excellent basket plants that should not be disturbed as long as appearance is maintained. Grow and propagate as for episcias.

GLOXINIA PERENNIS

This admirable species performs equally well in pots and in shaded garden beds. Plants grow to 30 cm (12 in) tall with glossy metallic copper foliage and large, mauve, scented blooms. After blooming, allow the plants to dry and tubers to form. The tubers should rest in the pots for about four months when they can be removed and potted in fresh moist soil when growth will begin again. Fertilize weekly with a product designed for flowering houseplants. Keep plants growing vigorously in bright filtered sunlight as the more top growth produced before blooming, the more flowers there will be. Propagate from tubers and seeds.

LIPSTICK PLANT *(Aechynanthus lobbianus)*
The Lipstick Plant is so called for its seasonal bloom of scarlet tubular flowers emerging in clusters from contrasting dark bases over glossy, rich, dark-green foliage. Raised as a basket specimen in bright overhead but indirect sunlight, the Lipstick Plant is valued in and out of bloom. Good light is needed for reliable bloom. These plants should not be disturbed as long as appearance is maintained. Propagate by cuttings and by division.

SINNINGIA CARDINALIS
Small specimens of this desirable plant carry clumps of bright red tubular, 2–5 cm (1–2 in) long flowers atop bright green leaves. Once stems have finished blooming, remove them to stimulate new shoots and more flowers. Plants will grow to 30–45 cm (12–18 in) in bright but indirect sunlight, indoors and out. Wick water and feed. Propagate from stem cuttings and from seeds.

***STREPTOCARPELLA SAXORUM* 'CONCORD BLUE'**
This plant has recently become popular as a basket specimen for lightly shaded, warm, humid locations. It can also be raised in a smaller, decorative pot, the rampant stems being pruned to keep growth bushy. Small, velvety leaves surround slender stalks of dainty blue-mauve flowers. Grow *Steptocarpella* in moist, slightly acid soil (pH 6.0–6.5). Feed continuously. Propagate from cuttings.

MORE CHOICES

- Columnea: trailing or upright plants for bright but indirect light. *Columnea microphylla* is recommended for baskets; flower colour ranges from scarlet through orange to yellow; propagate from cuttings.

Herbaceous plants – annuals and perennials

Herbaceous flowering plants are the mainstay of outdoor container displays. Movable tubs and baskets of brilliantly coloured plants at their peak of perfection can be assembled on stage, set against a permanent backdrop of trees and shrubs. Foliage plants chosen for their adaptability to often low light conditions are central to interior decoration. To have flowers produced indoors requires special attention to adequate lighting. As plants have variable growth rates, this should be kept in mind when combining different kinds and cultivars in any situation.

SELECTIONS FOR SUNNY LOCATIONS

BIDENS

Cascades of bright yellow flowers are the hallmark of this new sun- and heat-tolerant introduction to container gardening. Trailing Bidens 'Golden Eye' and 'Gold Marie' can be used in hanging baskets alone or in combination with other annuals such as brightly coloured, heat-tolerant Surfinia® or Supertunia™ petunias. Bidens seeds require light to germinate. To create a truly eye catching display, plant a minimum of 25 seedlings in and around a 40 cm (16 in) diameter wire basket. Plants bloom about six to eight weeks from sowing. Keep moist and feed regularly with additional, occasional application of chelated iron. Propagate the most vigorous and bushy individuals by tip cuttings.

BRUGMANSIA *(Datura)*

The white-flowered Angel's Trumpet is well known for garden accent value but more colourful introductions have greatly increased design opportunities for the adventurous gardener. Brugmansias make stunning additions to a large sunny patio. Hybrid *B*. × *insignis* 'Charles Grimaldi' bears huge, pendulous single yellow blooms amidst serrated foliage. Double yellow-flowered 'Golden Queen' can be easily grown from seed as can *B. sanguinea* which has spectacular 20 cm (8 in) long orange trumpets, and *B. suaveolens* 'Jamaica Yellow' with apricot blooms. These plants can become quite large, reaching 2 m (6 ft) in height and 3 m (10 ft) breadth at maturity. Grow large specimens in 50 cm (20 in) diameter clay pots or in deep tubs. Support the pots with decorative stones or blocks or with pots of foliage plants to prevent tipping the top-heavy specimens in high wind. For a more compact patio plant, try 'Double Eryngium Blue' with double ruffled bluish mauve trumpets amidst soft blue-green foliage. This cultivar grows to just over 1 m (3 ft) in height and may be raised from seed. All Brugmansias bloom best when grown in full sun. Soil should be rich but well drained. *ALL PARTS OF THESE PLANTS ARE POISONOUS.*

CLEOME

Cleome or Spider Flower is a tall annual perhaps not thought of as a typical container subject but useful when planted as a temporary screen. Open-textured Cleomes blend well with potted grasses such as Fountain Grass (*Pennisetum setaceum*). Grow cultivars such as white 'Helen Campbell', or violet 'Violet Queen', singly or as a blend. Pre-chill seed in the refrigerator for five days before sowing directly into a raised bed or in tubs. Thin seedlings to 30–40 cm (12–16 in) apart. Transplant any extra seedlings to garden beds when the seedlings are 10 cm (4 in) tall. Expect flowers within three months of sowing.

NICOTIANA

The fragrance and beauty of nicotiana blossoms is an invaluable asset to those looking for plants to be placed near entrances or on patios. Cultivars range in size from 30 cm up to 1 m (1–3 ft) and offer a range of colour from white through crimson, pink and even lime green. The fine seed needs light to germinate: plants bloom six weeks from seed. Choose the miniature-growing Merlin Series for smaller pots, compact Domino Series for planters and the taller Nicki Series for larger tubs. Heat-tolerant nicotianas will bloom best in full sun.

MARIGOLD (*Tagetes*)

Marigolds such as 'Antigua' that are not day-length sensitive are ideal for growing in the tropics where day length does not vary much year-round. Start such marigolds from seed at any time of the year. Tip cuttings may be taken to increase plants with particular appeal. Miniature, single-flowered *Tagetes* such as 'Starfire' provide a veritable glowing mass of blossoms above finely divided foliage. These compact beauties can be planted into the top and sides of a deep, moss-lined basket to enhance the cascade effect. Transplant seedlings to containers four weeks after sowing. Expect flowers ten weeks from seeds. Grow in full sun.

MORNING GLORY (*Ipomoea, Convolvulus*)

Variegated foliage and flowers coloured red, blue and pink are artfully combined in the Bush Convolvulus or Dwarf Morning Glory. Cultivars 'Blue Ensign' and 'Royal Marine' are recommended, blooming 60 days from seed. Raise in full sun to light shade. Since seedlings are difficult to transplant, sow seeds directly into a 30 cm (12 in) wide basket filled with moist, light soil mix. Pre-soaking seeds overnight will hasten germination. Propagate from seed.

PETUNIA

Larger-flowered petunias can be damaged by heavy tropical rain but smaller multiflora introductions such as 'Purple Wave' resist rain damage, producing masses of brilliantly coloured 5 cm (2 in) blooms on plants measuring a mere 15 cm (6 in) high yet spreading up to 60 cm (2 ft) across. Plant four to six plants of multiflora Petunia seedlings to a basket for an explosion of bloom, 12 to 14 weeks from sowing.

VERBENA

Deliciously fragrant, heat-tolerant, perennial verbenas such as the vibrant 'Homestead Purple', 'Taylortown Red' and 'Blue Wave' are exciting basket plants for sunny locations. These plants have two potential problems easily solved by good culture. Verbenas are susceptible to powdery mildew and spider mite attack especially if they are stressed by not being grown in full sun or if the soil becomes at all soggy. Planting Verbenas only in porous compost and careful watering will do much to avoid pest problems but if mites persist an insecticidal soap spray should keep them at bay. Verbenas may be raised from seed. Propagate selected plants by tip cuttings. Cuttings will root within 7–10 days under warm, humid conditions. Plant about four rooted cuttings per 25–30 cm (10–12 in) basket. Grow in full sun. Pinch once after the plants have become established. Expect masses of bloom in about 7–10 weeks. As blooming subsides, shear the plants lightly to promote side branching and more flowers.

ZINNIA

What better choice for a planter or a hanging basket on a sunny patio than the multiflowered, single *Zinnia angustifolia* 'Crystal White' or the equally stunning cultivar, 'Star Gold'. Blooming just 60 days from seed, these robust, heat-tolerant annuals thrive in full sun. Soil should be well drained and never permitted to become soggy.

MORE CHOICES FOR SUN

- Calico Plant (*Alternathera ficoidea*) 'Bettzickiana': less than 30 cm (1 ft) high; used as edging for tubs and raised beds; foliage coloured variously red, pink, bronze, green and yellow; propagate by tip cuttings.
- Calico Plant (*Alternathera ficoidea*) 'Snowball': less than 30 cm (1 ft) high; used as edging for tubs and raised beds or in a hanging basket; leaves green with white tips; propagate by tip cuttings.

- Cigar Plant (*Cuphea micropetala*): brilliant orange, hummingbird-pollinated tubular flowers on a 1.5 m (5 ft) high bushy plant; raise in 25 cm (10 in) pot; propagate from seed.
- Cosmos 'Ladybird': drought-tolerant; 30 cm (1 ft) tall annual; red, yellow or orange flowers; propagate from seed.
- Crossandra: can attain 2 m (6 ft) but best kept compact by raising new plants from freshly rooted cuttings; salmon, red ('Florida Flame'), coral, orange and yellow ('Florida Summer'); propagate from cuttings and from seeds.
- Firecracker Plant (*Cuphea ignea*) 'David Verity': 5 cm (2 in) long tubular scarlet flowers upon a 1.2 m (4 ft) high bushy plant; raise in 25 cm (10 in) pot; propagate from rooted tip cuttings or seed.
- Four O'Clock (*Mirabilis*): drought-tolerant; 1 m (3 ft) tall; multi-coloured flowers; pots or tubs; propagate from seed or by division.
- Globe Amaranth (*Gomphrena*) 'Gnome', 'Buddy': drought-tolerant; 25 cm (10 in) tall annual; pink, lavender, white; pots; propagate from seed.
- Golden Water Zinnia (*Wedelia trilobata* 'Outenreath Gold'): three-lobed leaves splashed gold on green and masses of yellow daisy blooms; large basket; sun; propagate by cuttings.
- Love-Lies-Bleeding (*Amaranthus caudatus*): drought-tolerant; 1.5 m (5 ft) tall annual; red or green long-lasting 'ropes' of bloom; tubs; propagate from seed.
- Melampodium: drought- and heat-tolerant annual; single yellow flowers; try 'Derby', 25 cm (10 in) tall.
- Pepper 'Thai Variegated': an edible hot pepper with striking white and pink variegated foliage and tumbling stems; baskets; propagate from cuttings.
- Periwinkle (*Catharanthus roseus*): 30 cm (12 in); 'Lemon Meringue' (white flowers and lemon-green foliage); 'Tropicana' (rose); 'Apricot Delight' (apricot pink); 'Parasol' (white with large red eye); 'Heat Wave' (deep rose flowers, branching habit); pots and tubs; propagate from cuttings and from seed which requires darkness to germinate.
- Portulaca 'Sundial': drought-tolerant; spreading annual; pots or baskets; all colours except blue; propagate from seed.
- Spanish Thyme (*Coleus amboinicus*) 'Ochre Flame': heavy, succulent two-toned green foliage; tub; culinary herb; propagate from cuttings.
- Variegated Spanish Thyme (*Coleus amboinicus*): green foliage edged white; striking hanging basket; culinary herb; propagate from cuttings.

SELECTIONS FOR PARTIAL OR FULL SHADE

BALSAM

Single-flowered Balsam (*Impatiens balsamifera*) is now found naturalized in many parts of the tropics. Double-flowered relatives of these colourful plants include extra dwarf 'Tom Thumb' which has 5 cm (2 in) wide flowers covering the top and sides of the 20 cm (8 in) tall stem. Colours range from white to pink, rose carmine, mauve and scarlet. The recently introduced 'Cajun' Series Impatiens is the perfect choice for hanging baskets set in hot, humid gardens. Tetraploid Impatiens 'Bruno' outperforms all others both in plant vigour and production of large, flat, substantial flowers. Balsams are reasonably drought-tolerant but perform best when well supplied with water. Seeds require light to germinate and will be adversely affected if temperatures during germination exceed 29 °C (86 °F). Keep seed trays out of direct sunlight. Transplant seedlings to their final container about two weeks after germination. Position seedlings 15 cm (6 in) apart for dwarf cultivars and 25 cm (10 in) apart with larger varieties. Expect flowers about 8 to 10 weeks after sowing. Grow with light overhead shade.

BROMELIADS

Of the many shapes, colours and sizes that can be found within this diverse group of plants, some are particularly suited to container culture in the home and garden. Clustering types such as the Tillandsias may be grown suspended from monofilament fishing line or wire, or mounted on pieces of wood. The glossy leaves of *Neoregelia* flush brilliant shades of red and mauve when these plants bloom but the flowers themselves are tiny and hidden. Miniature Earth Stars (*Cryptanthus*) make interesting pot plants and excellent additions to large terrariums. The Pineapples (*Ananas*), far from being merely food plants, have also been developed as decorative garden plants. Variegated cultivars are particularly sought after and prized when they produce exquisitely patterned miniature pineapples. *Aechmea fasciata* is equally admired for the showy, 50 cm (20 in) long pink inflorescence and blue flowers.

Bromeliads are easy to cultivate. Terrestrial kinds such as *Cryptanthus* are planted in porous soil while the epiphytes such as *Tillandsia* perform best when mounted on bark. Root systems are rarely substantial. Plant bromeliads in a mixture of equal parts of soil, compost and coarse sand. When watering or feeding these plants, wet the foliage as well as the soil. The leafy cups of bromeliads such as *Aechmea* and *Neoregelia* should be kept filled with rainwater. Indoors, especially in air-conditioned homes where humidity is low, mist the plants frequently. Propagate bromeliads by offsets and from seeds.

BROWALLIA

Browallia is a colourful South American plant suitable for pots, boxes and hanging baskets in semi-shaded patios and balconies. Height varies from 15 to 50 cm (6–20 in) according to the cultivar. Plants of the Starlight Series stand a mere 15 cm (6 in) tall at maturity. Blue or white blossoms appear 15–22 weeks after sowing. Seeds need light to germinate. Protect plants from strong sunlight and hot, drying wind. Pinch to encourage branching and re-blooming.

GERBERA

Gerberas (Transvaal Daisy) are prized for their long-lasting, brilliantly coloured blooms. They grow best in well-drained sandy loam and prefer cool nights (16 °C) which may be difficult to achieve in the lowland tropics but are attainable at higher elevations. The plants are particularly susceptible to crown rot, especially if planted too deep with soil covering the crown. Plant gerberas with the crown slightly above the soil surface. Surround the leaf rosette with coarse perlite or gravel. The Skipper Series are compact plants well suited to pot and container culture. The Festival Series are quicker to bloom, needing just 90 to 100 days from seed to flowering with many blooms per plant in shades of orange, red, yellow, rose and white. Provide light overhead shade. Seeds require light to germinate.

WISHBONE FLOWER

The Wishbone flower (*Torenia*) is an interesting and colourful compact pot plant for use in and around a lightly shaded patio. Colours in the 'Clown' series range from white with yellow or pink markings to light and dark pink, mauve and navy blue. *Torenia flava* 'Suzie Wong' is quite different having golden yellow flowers with rich dark throats and a trailing habit. 'Suzie Wong' can certainly brighten a shaded corner of the patio. Germinate seeds in total darkness. Raise plants in light to moderate shade. Torenias flower about 12 weeks from sowing.

Tip! Coleus cultivars vary as to the amount of sun they can manage. One way to test how much sun particular cultivars can withstand is to expose young, well-rooted plants gradually to more and more light until some show signs of distress such as colour bleaching. Those kinds without leaf problems are obviously more sun-tolerant.

MORE CHOICES FOR PARTIAL OR FULL SHADE

- Anthurium: 30–100 cm (12–36 in); bright diffuse light; moist, organic compost; 'Powys Pride' (deep pink spathes and white splashed foliage), 'Red Elf' (miniature with double red spathes); propagate by division.
- Blue Ginger (*Dichorisandra thrysiflora variegata*): 2 m (6 ft); stout succulent stems with silver-streaked, glossy, spirally-arranged foliage and 15 cm (6 in) long heads of riveting blue flowers; juvenile foliage more distinctly patterned; semi-shade; moist; tub; propagate by division.
- Calathea: 30 cm (12 in); plants with very colourful foliage; *C. fasciata* (silvery blotches on broad green leaves), *C. majestica* 'Albolineata' (white leaves having green midribs and veins), *C. picturata* 'Argentea' (green leaves with broad white centre patch), *C. roseo-picta* 'Asian Beauty' (rose purple brushed generously over silvery leaves, narrow green edge); filtered sunlight or light shade; propagate by division.
- Coleus: 25–100 cm (10–36 in) tall; leaves multicoloured or in separate colours; full sun to semi-shade depending upon cultivar; pots or tubs; pinch out growing point to keep plants bushy; propagate from seed or by cuttings of selected plants.
- Dieffenbachia: handsome leafy plants worth while for interior use where the showy foliage will be less likely damaged by slugs; *D. amoena* (dark-green leaves mottled white), 'Camille' and 'Tropic Marianne' (creamy yellow leaves bordered green), 'Rudolph Roehrs' (white blotches on golden green leaves, midrib and leaf edges dark green); take cuttings or marcots before plants become leggy; propagate from cuttings and by air layering.
- Dwarf Shrimp Plant (*Justicia brandegeana* 'Jambalaya'): compact form of the common shrimp plant; foliage dark to reddish green depending upon available light; long-lasting shrimp-coloured bracts persist long after white tubular flowers are over; pots; propagate by cuttings.
- Dwarf Variegated Shell Ginger (*Alpinia speciosa* (Zerumbet)): lovely gold and green, dwarf version of a popular garden plant; pots and tubs; light shade; propagate by division.
- Fittonia: red, pink or silver net-veined creeping plants for use in terrariums or in shady, humid ferneries; propagate by cuttings.
- Foxtail Asparagus (*Asparagus densiflorus*) 'Meyers': 60 cm (2 ft) long bushy stems; pots or baskets; propagate by seed or division.
- Giant Moth Ginger (*Hedychium hasseltii*): 75 cm (30 in) tall; large, white, fragrant flowers over broad, heavy foliage; bright, filtered sunlight; pots; propagate by division.

- Guzmania 'Empire': 40 cm tall bromeliad having a showy whorl of scarlet bracts and orange-red flowers in the plant centre; pots; mounted; propagate by offsets.
- Impatiens 'Mini-Hawaiian Hawaii': tiny pink and white blooms massed on a ball of similar size foliage; partial shade to full sun depending upon local conditions; pots; propagate by cuttings.
- Ivory Stepladder Plant (*Costus dubius*): showy dark-green leaves boldly striped white; tubs; light shade; propagate by division.
- Prayer Plant (*Maranta leuconeura*): lovely matt foliage that folds upwards at dusk; leaves variably marked brown on green or in 'Erythrophylla', veined red over olive brown; bright indirect light; shallow pots and baskets; propagate by cuttings and by division.
- Sprenger Asparagus (*Asparagus densiflorus* 'Sprengeri'): 1 m (3 ft) long stems; pot on a pedestal, baskets; propagate from seed or division.
- *Syngonium podophyllum*: to 50 cm (20 in); showy foliage; 'Lemon & Lime' (green leaves with striking white veining), 'Bob White' (leaves almost entirely white); bright indirect light with more light for heavily variegated cultivars; pots and baskets; propagate from cuttings.
- Vriesea 'Poelmanii': 30 cm tall bromeliad; rosette of shining green leaves; 60 cm tall scarlet, sword-like inflorescence; bright indirect to filtered sunlight; humidity essential; propagate from offsets.

Orchids

Orchids, especially those species and hybrids that are very floriferous or fragrant and those with very showy or long-lasting blooms, are prized for growing in baskets or for mounting on pieces of wood or bark. These orchids may be grown and flower where they are to be viewed or raised elsewhere and moved to the reception area only when in peak bloom.

Some orchids will bloom year-round but most flower only seasonally in response to changes in rainfall, day length and/or night temperature. Orchids are generally more tolerant of dryness than of continual dampness. Roots can decay if the potting medium is not perfectly drained. With a few exceptions, orchids are intolerant of salt and especially of sodium in the water supply. When fertilizing orchids, apply weak feedings frequently as opposed to heavy, infrequent applications. For any plants not exposed to rainfall, alternate fertilizer applications with plain water to control the build-up of mineral salts in the containers. Orchids grow best with some shade but the degree of shade needed is very much dependent upon the plant and the local climatic conditions. Leaves accustomed to partial shade can easily burn if exposed abruptly to strong sunlight. Alternatively, plants raised in a shade house can more easily adjust to placement in a home for several weeks. It is best to wait until most flower buds have opened before moving plants as relocation can interfere with the elegant and orderly display of blooms.

Almost any orchid can be moved indoors for temporary display. Some orchids may be grown permanently indoors in filtered sunlight. The Moth orchids (*Phalaenopsis*, *Doritaenopsis*) and tropical Lady's-slippers (*Paphiopedilum*) grow and bloom well in subdued light, making them ideal candidates for indoor use. Both types have long-lasting flowers and pleasing foliage.

Orchids are propagated by seed, by division and by the removal of rooted offsets.

BRASSAVOLA NODOSA

Lady-of-the-Night is the popular name for this night-fragrant white-flowered orchid which grows well in a hanging basket. Situate these orchids where their night fragrance will be appreciated. Plants may bloom several times a year. Hybrids of *B. nodosa* such as *Bc.* Binosa (green with spots), *Bl.* Richard Mueller (yellow with spots) and *Potinara* Hoku Gem (yellow changing to orange) have similar cultural requirements but provide a colourful variety. All of this group grow well in bright situations with some overhead shade from the midday sun. They are drought-tolerant but thrive with supplementary watering during the driest times. Propagate by division.

CATTLEYA SKINNERI 'HETTIE JACOBS'

This tetraploid cultivar is superior in flower colour and size to the typical species form. Plants can be raised to immense size provided the potting mix permits perfect drainage even to the centre of the clump. Support must be adequate to manage what must eventually become a very heavy basket. This orchid produces clusters of purple flowers in March to May. Propagate by division.

ONCIDIUM AMPLIATUM

One of the popular 'Bee' orchids, this species provides a wealth of bright golden yellow flowers in March to May. Substantial sprays are produced by even modest plants. A 50 cm (20 in) diameter wire basket filled with chunky pieces of bark will support the growth of a large plant. Propagate by division.

PHALAENOPSIS AND DORITAENOPSIS

Moth orchids come in shades of white, pink and yellow, with or without spots and stripes. Many long-lasting blooms are evenly arrayed along long arching stems. The broad, green to reddish-green leaves are easily sun-burned. Propagate by offsets.

VANDA AND ASCOCENDA

If there is an orchid that provides flowers in all colours of the rainbow, it is the hybrid vanda or ascocenda. Vandas have the largest blooms, some reaching the size of a saucer. The best cultivars have sturdy stems bearing many flat, colourful flowers of heavy substance. Such blooms will remain in good condition for several months. Ascocendas are hybrid orchids combining the shape and size of *Vanda* blooms with the more diminutive plant size and brilliant colours of *Ascocentrum*. Hybrids are compact with multiple sprays of proportionately smaller, but more brightly coloured blooms. Both vandas and ascocendas are easily raised in hanging baskets made of wooden slats. Little or no potting medium is needed with adult plants. Roots are numerous and lengthy, hanging down beneath the basket. These should not be removed. Raise vandas and ascocendas with light to moderate overhead shade, broad-leaved plants requiring more shade than plants having more folded or terete foliage. Water roots daily except during the rainy season. Propagate by top cuttings and by removal of offsets.

MORE CHOICES

- Reed Stem Orchid (*Epidendrum radicans variegatum*): a Japanese introduction having yellow striped leaves; stems topped with heads of scarlet blooms; full sun; tubs; propagate from offsets. Seed-raised plants may or may not be variegated.
- *Broughtonia sanguinea*: Jamaican native plant which adapts readily to basket culture. Many hybrids now in cultivation maintain the compact habit and long inflorescence style of the species. Propagate by division.

Palms and cycads

There are many palms and cycads that lend themselves to container planting. Confining roots within a limited space controls growth. Clustering specimens are particularly useful as are those with interesting foliage. The Lady Palm, the Clustered Fishtail Palm, and the

Reed Palms grow well in partial shade, the Reed and Lady Palms being especially suited to interior use. The Coontie is a cycad relative eminently suited to container culture outdoors in semi-shade to full sun locations. The plant is naturally short and bushy. Palms, cycads and their relatives are best propagated from freshly collected seeds.

To maintain their appearance, container-grown palms require some protection from wind. Newly planted specimens especially should be sheltered until roots become established. Raise palms and cycads in coarse garden soil with added compost. Acid-soil-loving species require an additional measure of well-rotted manure and compost added to the mix. The chosen container should be heavy to balance tall and possibly top-heavy specimens. Once a container becomes filled with roots, the plant will rise up out of it. This is the signal to re-pot the plant. Fertilize plants about four times a year using a product containing chelated trace minerals. Never allow the roots to dry out but also beware of sogginess caused by pots sitting in saucers of water.

Indoors, palms and cycads will grow more slowly and therefore watering and fertilizer application frequency should be adjusted accordingly. Plants placed in bright, sunlit areas will require more water than those growing away from windows.

> *Tip!* To have pots full of fresh palm foliage, plant 6 to 12 palm seeds together in the same container.

The first sign of palm and cycad distress will be yellowing foliage. Dead roots resulting from either too much or too little water, nutrient imbalance, pests or diseases can be the cause. Palms especially may be afflicted by diseases such as Lethal Yellowing.

CARDBOARD PALM *(Zamia furfuracea (pumila))*
This plant is not a true palm but a cycad relative having hard, dark-green leaves and leaflets coated underneath with a thick golden-brown fleece. As the plant matures, the thick trunk becomes apparent. Grow in filtered sunlight.

COONTIE *(Zamia floradana)*
Dark-green feathery leaves are produced in flushes to form a low bush about 1 m (3 ft) high and wide. Mature plants produce rusty-brown cones in the centre of the plant. Salt-tolerant Coontie is recommended for lightly shaded gardens near the sea.

FIJI FAN PALM *(Pritchardia pacifica)*
Large, deeply folded, fan-shaped leaves of this palm are covered with a white fluffy coating when young. The leaves dominate the plant. While this palm will thrive if grown in full sun, a more handsome specimen is obtained if the palm is raised in shade away from intense midday sun and protected from drying wind.

FISHTAIL PALM *(Caryota mitis)*
The Clustered Fishtail Palm prefers rich, acidic soil. It can be grown in full sun once mature but should be sheltered when young. The name comes from the characteristically shaped foliage. Bright red fruits irritate the skin if handled.

KENTIA OR SENTRY PALM *(Howea fosteriana)*
The Kentia Palm will thrive in full sun to partial shade. Handsome feathery leaves arch proudly, giving a stately appearance. Soil should be well drained.

LADY PALM *(Rhapis excelsa)*
The Lady Palm is delicate, reaching just over 1 m (3 ft) in height. Each leaf is composed of four to eight, blunt-tipped, glossy green leaflets. The slender trunks are covered in the netlike remnants of old leaf bases. This palm thrives in high humidity and grows best on a sheltered, lightly shaded patio. Selected cultivars are available from specialist nurseries.

REED PALM *(Chamaedorea)*
The Reed Palms such as *Chamaedorea seifrizii* have clustering stems decked with elegant feathery foliage. This palm performs best in the shade and is recommended for interior use.

MORE CHOICES

Cycads

- *Encephalartos ferox*: 1–2 m (3–6 ft) diameter rosette; a dazzling specimen with glossy dark-green leaves having holly-like leaflets; cinnamon brown cones; full sun to light shade.
- *Encephalartos munchii*: palm-like rosette 1–2 m (3–6 ft) diameter; mid-green leathery foliage; large, handsome cones; full sun to light shade.

Palms

- Golden Palm (*Chrysalidocarpus lutescens*): 2 m (6 ft); clustering golden stems having graceful, arching feathery leaves; full sun to semi-shade; plant several seedlings to a pot for quick mass effect.
- Round Leaf Palm (*Licuala grandis*): 2 m (6 ft); glossy green, rounded fan-shaped leaves with notched margins; leaves arch gracefully; accent plant for a sheltered patio.

Shrubs and trees

Shrubs and trees are some of the largest plants other than palms and vines that may be grown outdoors in containers. Selection and placement of large plants must be carefully considered as part of the overall landscape design. Plants may be selected to provide a focal accent, shade, a privacy screen or to disguise something like a pool pump. Pots and tubs may be arranged singly or in groups of the same or different kinds or cultivars. Select plants for the purpose intended. If a screen is needed, choose quick growing shrubs such as oleander or crape myrtle. If an accent specimen is wanted, select plants which have landscape value in or out of bloom. An alternative is to rotate accent plants, removing those past their prime and replacing them with different plants raised elsewhere. Limit the number of unusual plants in any one area. Balance brilliant colour with a more benign backdrop. Place variegated foliage plants such that each specimen may be admired for its particular attributes.

BAUHINIA

A group of small to medium-sized trees and shrubs, many of which are suited to be patio specimens. All have showy flowers and distinctive, two-lobed leaves. Grow bauhinias in full sun, in tubs containing slightly acidic soil. Prune once flowering is finished. Propagate from seed.

- Nasturtium Bauhinia (*B. galpinii*): loads of coral flowers are produced from a modest shrub growing up to 2 m (6 ft). Prune to keep bushy and floriferous.
- Mountain Ebony or Orchid Tree (*B. variegata* (*purpurea*)): this small tree grows to 3 m (10 ft) and often has several trunks. It can be selectively pruned to have one trunk or be permitted to grow as a clump. Flowers are a rich purplish pink.

BIRD CATCHER TREE *(Pisonia brunoniana* 'Variegata'*)*
This modest, slow-growing tree is known for its very sticky seeds. The variegated form is admired for the marbled satin leaves in shades of green and cream: new growth is coppery pink. Regular pruning will force the production of colourful new shoots. One need never endure the sticky seeds if the tree is kept pruned. With all the pruning, it will be important to feed monthly and never to permit the tree to be stressed for lack of water. Grow this plant in light shade. Propagate from semi-hardwood and hardwood cuttings.

BANANAS
Several dwarf bananas have ornamental value because their foliage is attractively marked or they produce interesting flowers and/or fruits. One of the smallest is *Musa velutina*, a mere 1.2–2 m (4–6 ft) tall. Upward facing pink infloresence bracts and flowers are followed by many inedible, fuzzy pink bananas. This species produces lots of seeds which should be harvested from ripe fruits and rinsed in plain water before sowing. Taller *Musa zebrina*, 2–3 m (6–10 ft) tall, is recommended for its striking mottled maroon on green foliage. Cultivar 'Dwarf Red' is not only compact at 1.2–2 m (4–6 ft) tall but also combines a showy maroon trunk and red-skinned fruits of excellent table quality. Broad green leaves sport a red midrib. Plant ornamental bananas in large tubs to accommodate clustering of pseudostems over several years. Raise in full sun but sheltered from strong wind. Propagate by offsets produced from the base of a plant that has borne fruit or from seed when present.

BOUGAINVILLEA *(see* Vines*)*

CHASTE TREE *(Vitex agnus-castus)*
Pleasantly aromatic, compound foliage topped with spikes of purple flowers combine to make this small tree a valuable plant for container gardening. It is somewhat salt-tolerant. Because the chaste tree blooms only on new growth, it responds well to heavy pruning immediately following the flowering period. A variegated leaf cultivar is used commercially. Raise this tree in a tub filled with porous soil and grow in full sun. It does poorly in soggy soil. Fertilize when in active growth. Propagate from semi-hardwood cuttings.

CITRUS
Oranges, lemons, limes, grapefruit and tangerines can all be grown in tubs as patio trees. Dwarf fruit trees remain compact because of a

specially chosen rootstock. Enquire locally as to which cultivars have been appropriately top grafted for your purpose. Prune the tree only above the graft, cutting back the leader shoot but leaving all side branches to create a bushy plant.

CRAPE MYRTLE *(Lagerstroemia)*
Small trees or shrubs, depending upon the cultivar chosen, crape myrtles are colourful flowering shrubs for drier tropical situations. Raise them in full sun with plenty of air movement to avoid damaging mildew. Once crape myrtle plants are well established, they are quite drought-tolerant. Miniature cultivars such as 'Baton Rouge' (red), 'Mardi Gras' (purple) and 'Pink Blush' are suited to cultivation in large clay pots. These miniature shrubs measure just over 1 m (3 ft) in all dimensions. Crape myrtles naturally produce multiple shoots. If desired, a plant can be trained to be a patio tree by diligently removing extra shoots and suckers. Prune the top to encourage branching once the desired height has been reached. These plants flower on new branches. Always prune immediately after blooming to avoid removal of flower-bud-bearing parts. Crape myrtles grow very quickly, especially if given a lot of water and fertilizer. Resist the urge to over-fertilize this plant. Slow-release fertilizers added to the initial soil mix will be sufficient to support the plant for a year or more depending upon rainfall. Propagate by semi-hardwood cuttings and from seed marketed under the series name 'Supersonic'. Seed requires light to germinate.

FRANGIPANI *(Plumeria)*
Frangipanis are popular garden trees, renowned for their range of flower colour and for their heavy perfume. A few dwarf cultivars including 'Key West Red', 'Dwarf Singapore White', and 'Petite Pink' are recommended for planting in tubs around a sunny patio where they will delight the eye by day and the nose by night. Plumerias are very drought-tolerant once established but are intolerant of soggy conditions and therefore should be planted only in a porous soil. Fertilize established trees every three months with a liquid fertilizer high in phosphorus and potassium such as 8 : 14 : 10 (N : P : K) with added micronutrients. Propagate by large cuttings rooted in sand.

GOLDEN DEWDROP *(Duranta repens)*
Also known as the Brazilian Skyflower, this vigorous shrub grows in multi-stemmed clumps of arching branches dangling lilac-blue flowers followed by yellow fruit. Grown in full sun to light shade,

this shrub may be trained as a patio tree. Heavy pruning once a year after the main flowering period will ensure the production of new branches from which flowers appear. Propagate by semi-hardwood cuttings.

HIBISCUS

Showy hibiscus produce a profusion of blooms year-round when raised in full sun in tubs of nematode-free, well-drained soil. Hibiscus responds well to periodic applications of chelated iron to prevent chlorosis. From the very wide range of cultivars available, consider the following for training as patio trees: 'San Diego Red', 'Cherie' (yellow with maroon throat), 'Fiesta' (orange changing over the day to white). For a strong, bushy growth habit, try 'Morning Glory' (blush pink) or 'Jason Okumoto' (semi-double gold with red). Prune to keep the bushy habit and to promote new growth from which flowers are produced. Propagate by bud grafting.

LANTANA

Bushy lantanas can be a mainstay of sunny seaside gardens. Floriferous, drought- and salt-tolerant cultivars make handsome pot plants or hanging baskets. Bush lantanas grow about 2 m (6 ft) high and wide. Plant cultivars such as 'American Red' and 'Christine' (pink) in 30 cm (12 in) diameter pots. Prune to maintain shape as a bush or select one stem and prune to have a ball of branches and flowers 30–60 cm (1–2 ft) above the container. Spreading lantanas are best suited to baskets. Choose cultivars such as 'Sunburst' or 'Cream Carpet'. Mauve flowered lantanas blend particularly well with variegated companion plants. Propagate by semi-hardwood cuttings.

MEXICAN HEATHER *(Cuphea hyssopifolia)*

Mexican Heather is a dainty shrub just 30 cm (12 in) tall and up to 60 cm (24 in) wide. The many branches are thick with tiny glossy green leaves and masses of flowers in mauve, rose or white. Raise this shrub in full sun to light shade. Plant in well-drained sandy soil in a 20 cm (8 in) diameter pot. Propagate from tip cuttings.

OLEANDER *(Nerium oleander)*

Drought- and salt-tolerant oleanders deserve a special place in sunny tropical gardens, especially those located near the sea. The advent of compact cultivars such as 'Petite Pink' and 'Marrakesh' (warm red) provides an opportunity to grow this sun-loving shrub in large pots or tubs in and around the patio or pool. Taller cultivars can be kept more compact through judicious pruning and by keeping them pot-bound. Flowers, which are produced at the tips of new branches, can be either single, semi- or fully double, and are sometimes fragrant. Colours range from pure white through all shades of pink, red, wine and yellow. Some cultivars have variegated foliage. Keep oleanders regularly pruned to encourage branching and subsequently more blooms. Pruning will also maintain the overall shape and control the size of the bush. Propagate by air-layering and by softwood or semi-hardwood cuttings.

MORE CHOICES

Shrubs

- *Acalypha wilkesiana* 'Kilauea' (Miniature Fire Dragon): dwarf, mounded cultivar having tiny twisted leaves coloured copper with a cream margin; pot; sun; propagate from cuttings.
- Arabian Jasmine (*Jasminium sambac*): 1 m (3 ft) high and wide; very fragrant double white flowers; tub; sun; propagate from cuttings.
- Blue Potato Shrub (*Solanum rantonnettii*): 2–3 m (6–10 ft) high and wide; rich blue-violet flowers; tub; sun; propagate from cuttings and from seed.
- Bottle Palm (Pony Tail Tree) (*Beaucarnea*): 2 m (6 ft) with age; drought-tolerant plants with stems which become swollen at the base with age; a mass of long, slender, curving leaves form a 'tail' at the top; give bright, indirect light; propagate from seeds.
- Bougainvillea
  double-flowered cultivars – Cherry Blossom, Manila Red, Tahitian Maid (pink)
  single-flowered cultivars – Purple Queen, Rosenka.
- Crape Myrtle (*Lagerstroemia indica*): 'Petite Embers' (rose red), 'Petite Plum', 'Petite Red Imp', 'Petite Snow'.
- Croton (*Codiaeum*): 2 m (6 ft); showy, multicoloured and interestingly shaped foliage; full sun to bright filtered sunlight; moist, fertile soil; propagate from cuttings and by air layering.
- Dracaena: 3 m (10 ft); leafy plants prized for graceful habit and colourful foliage; very bright but indirect light best to maintain variegated *D. marginata* cultivars and selected showy varieties of *D. terminalis*; youngest foliage is the most colourful; keep a fresh appearance by starting new plants from cuttings or marcots.

- Glory Bush (*Tibouchina urvilleana*): 3–4 m (10–13 ft) high and up to 2 m (6 ft) wide; huge satiny purple flowers; velvety bronze-green foliage; moist, fertile soil in tubs; some shade; propagate by softwood cuttings.
- Golden Dewdrop, Brazilian Sky Flower (*Duranta repens*): multi-stemmed, 3–4 m (10–13 ft) high and wide; sky-blue flowers, golden fruits. Look also for the as yet unidentified dwarf cultivar with rich lilac blooms, known as 'Hansoti No. 26'; pots and tubs; sun; propagate from cuttings and seeds.
- Ixora 'Sunkist': 75 cm (30 in) tall; apricot blooms and glossy foliage cover this compact bush; pots; sun; propagate from cuttings.
- Lantana (*L. camara*): 'Greg Grant' (light yellow, two-tone leaves); 'Samantha' (golden yellow, variegated); pots and tubs; sun; propagate from cuttings.
- Ming Aralia (*Polyscias fruticosa*): to 1 m (3 ft) with age; fine green foliage in clusters on slow-growing branches; propagate from cuttings.
- Pride of Barbados, Dwarf Poinciana (*Caesalpinia pulcherrima*): 3 m (10 ft) tall; quick growing shrub for tubs; for screening or acting as a light windbreak; sun; propagate from seeds.
- Surinam Powder Puff (*Calliandra surinamensis*): 3 m (10 ft) tall; pink puffs of flowers against delicate lacy foliage; sun; propagate from seeds or from cuttings.

Trees

- Frangipani (*Plumeria*): 'Candy Stripe' (white and yellow stripes on red flowers); 'Bridal White' (fragrant white flowers in large clusters on a bushy plant); 'Petite Pink' (pale pink flowers on a naturally dwarf plant); 'Dwarf Singapore White' (densely branched dwarf plant having clusters of white flowers with a lemony fragrance); 'Pompano Pink' (large deep pink flowers on a compact, upright tree); 'Yellow Jack' (large lemony yellow flowers on a vigorous, compact tree); tubs; sun; propagate from cuttings.
- Raja Coral Tree (*Erythrina humeana* 'Raja'): 3 m (10 ft) high by 2 m (6 ft) wide; clusters of stunning red flowers on a seasonally deciduous tree; trilobed foliage; tubs; sun; propagate from seeds.
- Weeping Fig Tree (*Ficus benjamina*) 'Reginald': two-toned, lime green on darker green, glossy foliage; light overhead shade; keep pruned to 2 m; propagate from cuttings or by air layering.

Fruit trees for tubs

(Choose top grafted stock for compact growth and quick fruit production.)

BANANA (Many ornamental bananas are now raised by tissue culture)

- Double (Mahoi): grows to just 2 m (6 ft), producing two or more bunches of delicious fruit; raise in a large, permanent tub; avoid dividing a clump as this will reduce the likelihood of a double crop.
- Ornata: light green foliage, pink petioles and a pink inflorescence followed by green bananas. Ornamental.
- Dwarf Red: 2 m (6 ft); stunning plant and fruit; green leaves with maroon midrib, wine-coloured pseudostem and fruit. Fruit interior orange and delicious when ripe.
- Velutina: 2 m (6 ft); compact showy plant having deep pink inflorescence followed by pink, seedy fruits; propagate from seed and by offsets.
- Blood Banana (*Musa zebrina*): 2 m (6 ft); magnificent maroon and green variegated foliage, leaves solid red beneath.

CITRUS
'Bearss Seedless Lime', 'Melogold' Grapefruit, 'Oroblanco' Grapefruit (drier regions), 'Minneola' Tangelo, 'Chandler' Pommelo, 'Star Ruby' Grapefruit, 'Dancy' Tangerine (hot, humid regions).

FIG
Black Jack Fig (*Ficus carica* 'Black Jack'): large dark-brown fruits with sweet deep pink flesh; keep pruned to 2 m (6 ft).

PINEAPPLE GUAVA *(Feijoa sellowiana)*
High humidity will interfere with pollination; needs 100–200 hours' exposure to 7 °C (45 °F) or less to flower and fruit; green skinned oval fruit, white flowers with bright red stamens in a showy tuft; flowers edible; full sun to partial shade; keep pruned to 3 m (10 ft). Recommended for higher elevations only.

STAR FRUIT *(Averrhoa carambola)*
Red and white flowers borne along branches followed by oblong, five-angled yellow fruit; selected cultivars have the best tasting fruit; seedlings begin to bear after three years.

Vines and twiners

Climbing plants offer an opportunity to explore the vertical garden dimension. Whether the plants chosen are herbaceous annual vines for a quick and showy effect or robust woody perennials able to deliver fabulous colour with a minimum of care, all can be accommodated in containers. Weaker, slender herbaceous vines should either be supported or be left to trail gracefully from baskets. Stronger climbers, such as the gloriosa lily which has leaf tendrils or philodendrons which can root on to the climbing support, perform well on a trellis with a minimum of care. For heavier woody vines and scrambling plants raised in tubs, an important consideration is supporting the stems with an appropriately constructed trellis. Bloom-laden branches of sprawling shrubs such as bougainvillea may either be supported against a wall or can simply be allowed to spill over an arch or low fence.

BLUE TRUMPET VINE *(Thunbergia grandiflora)*
Pendant racemes of mid-blue flowers cascade year-round from this spectacular woody vine. While the vine can be more than 5 m (16 ft) long, it is easily trained to grow on a trellis over an entry or even on long wires holding a substantial hanging basket where the flowers can be viewed from below. Prune once or twice yearly to promote production of new shoots and more blooms. Propagate from hardwood cuttings and offsets taken from the base of the vine.

CLOCKVINE *(Thunbergia alata)*
The orange-flowered, herbaceous clockvine is a charming addition to a window box or a hanging basket. The 'Suzie' series provides variety in flower colour from white, yellow to orange, with or without a contrasting 'eye'. Plant clockvines in moisture-retentive soil and feed regularly. Raise in full sun to light shade. Do not pinch or prune. Propagate from seed.

MOONFLOWER *(Calonyction)*
Perennial climbers such as the fragrant white moonflower can be used effectively in large containers positioned in full sun beneath 2–4 m (6–13 ft) high trellis. Pre-soaking seeds overnight will hasten germination. Sow seeds where the plants are to grow, 2 cm (1 in) deep. Plants will begin blooming after 8–10 weeks. Fragrant white flowers open at sunset, closing by noon the following day. Assemble guests on the patio for the moment when the buds open for an awe-inspiring treat.

MORE CHOICES

For sun

- Bougainvillea: drought-tolerant; 2–3 m (6–10 ft) long branches; 'Purple Queen', 'Rosenka' (gold to pink); double-flowered cultivars – Cherry Blossom, Manila Red, Tahitian Maid (pink); large basket or tub; propagate from cuttings.
- Bougainvillea: 'Royal Bengal Red' (red bracts against variegated foliage); 'Raspberry Ice' (naturally low growing with bright pink bracts and ivory-edged leaves); propagate from cuttings.
- Crimson Passionflower (*Passiflora vitifolia*): 4–5 m (12–16 ft) long twining stems; edible fruit; basket or tub; propagate from seed.
- Spanish Jasmine (*Jasminium grandiflorum*): 1–1.5 m (3–5 ft) long branches; very fragrant white flowers; basket or tub, propagate from cuttings.
- Watermelon Leaf Passionflower (*Passiflora cuspidifolia*): 1 m (3 ft) long stems; pale-veined, purplish-green leaves and intriguing flowers on a compact twining plant suited to dappled sunlight; trellis in pot or basket; propagate from seed.

For partial or full shade

- Variegated Australian Jasmine (*Jasminium volubile* 'Mediopicta'): 2 m (6 ft) long branches; white flowers; yellow-spotted leaves; basket or tub; propagate from cuttings.
- Mandevilla (*Mandevilla sanderi*): 2–2.7 m (6–8 ft) long twining branches; 'Red Riding Hood' (deep rose pink); hanging basket; propagate from cuttings.
- Mandevilla: 5–7 m (16–23 ft) long twining stems; 'Alice du Pont' (light pink); 'Summer Snow' (white); tub with trellis; propagate from cuttings.

Water plants

What better way to cast off daily stress than to gaze at water plants in and around a limpid pool. Water gardens do not have to be immense ponds with streams and water platters (*Victoria amazonica*). A large impervious pot will serve as home for miniature waterlilies or dwarf lotus. Even vigorous and sometimes invasive floating water hyacinth and water lettuce will grow in proportion to a container if care is taken to limit mineral nutrients. Water depth can be critical for certain plants. Water cannas, lotus and umbrella sedges prefer shallow water while waterlilies need sufficient water over the rhizome to float their leaves and flowers. Blooming plants require at least six hours of sunshine daily. All water plants except floating specimens should be planted in heavy, rich soil. Weight the soil and rhizome with stones. Fertilize with slow-release tablets especially manufactured for use with pool plants. Propagate by division, by offsets where present or from seed.

LOTUS *(Nelumbo)*

Some varieties of lotus are giants standing 2 m (6 ft) tall. They could easily overwhelm a pond but alone in tubs they lend a dramatic accent to a bend in the garden path or give an exotic touch to an entry way. Choose more dwarf growing cultivars such as double pink 'Momo Botan' or double white, fragrant Tulip Lotus (Shirokunshi) for 25 L (5 gal) water pots. Group pots of blooming plants in full sun beside a pool for a mass effect.

SEDGE *(Cyperus)*

Dwarf Umbrella Plant (*Cyperus haspans*): this compact sedge is useful as an accent plant in combination with floating plants such as miniature waterlilies. Plant in pots of shallow water or in very moist soil. This cultivar reaches 45–60 cm (1.5–2 ft). It tolerates some shade.

SNOWFLAKES *(Nymphoides)*

Both the White Snowflake (*N. indica*) and the Yellow Snowflake (*N. geminata*) with their mottled reddish brown and green diminutive foliage and dainty fringed blooms are perfectly proportioned for small, shallow water gardens. Propagate by division.

WATER HYACINTH *(Eichornia)*

The water hyacinth is indisputably magnificent in bloom but can become a menace to waterways if it escapes cultivation. It does, however, float happily under control in small water pots, pools and impervious tubs where it will delight the eye with its inflated leaf stems and gorgeous blooms. Withhold fertilizer to control vigour and growth. Propagate by division.

WATER LETTUCE *(Pistia)*

Velvety lime-green leaves arranged gracefully in a floating rosette are the reason for the common name. Like the water hyacinth, this plant can easily become invasive if allowed to escape cultivation. It reproduces by stolons. Tiny versions of the parent plant break away and these may be used to effect in a miniature water garden.

These plants grow so quickly and in such profusion that once individuals become too large they may simply be removed and replaced with one or several of their offsets! Withhold fertilizer to control growth.

WATERLILIES *(Nymphaea)*

Among the many waterlily cultivars are some that are admirably suited for small ponds or tubs. Provide 15–50 cm (6–20 in) of water over the growing points and sufficient space to float leaves and flowers. Ensure that the plants receive a minimum of six hours' sunshine daily to have continuous bloom. For a pond with about 1 square metre surface area (11 square feet), choose among compact cultivars such as 'Panama Pacific' (purple) and 'Mrs Martin E. Randig' (deep blue). For even smaller water gardens in 25 L (5 gal) tubs, consider 'Helvola' (yellow) or its sport 'Joanne Pring' (pink). Plant separate tubs of each cultivar or establish both cultivars in the same small pond together with umbrella sedges in the background for vertical accent. Waterlilies will profit from feeding with slow-release tablets especially formulated for water plants. Propagate by division.

MORE CHOICES

- Arrowroot (*Canna concinna*): showy foliage topped with scarlet blooms on a compact plant; plant in shallow water.
- Mosaic Plant (*Ludwigia sidioides*): 8 cm (3 in) wide rosettes of red and green foliage; plant 15 cm (6 in) deep; plant spreads 60 cm (2 ft).
- Waterlily 'Colorata': a pygmy species having lilac-blue flowers in abundance; excellent for small water gardens.
- Waterlily 'Margaret Mary': a pale blue-flowered beauty that is at home in a small water garden.
- Waterlily 'Texas Dawn': a dwarf plant with speckled leaves and white flowers.

Floating plants

- Variegated Chinese Water Chestnut (*Eleocharis dulcis* 'Variegata'): narrow leaves sport a central yellow stripe; plant in moist soil or a shallow water garden.
- Variegated Waffle Plant (*Hemigraphis* 'Exotica'): a creeping, purple-leaved plant; metallic effect punctuated by yellow blotches; for a small, shallow pool; semi-shade; propagate by cuttings.

- Water Amaranth (*Alternathera polygonoides*): an interesting, slender, purplish-leaved plant.
- Water Poppy (*Hydrocleys nymphoides*): round shiny leaves, up to 7.5 cm (3 in) wide; yellow flowers.

Appendix I
Suggestions for Bonsai-style Culture

Alternathera (*Alternathera ficoidea*) 'Christmas Tree': cute tree-like plants with grey-green foliage.

Asparagus (*Asparagus crispus*): arched stems with tiny leaves and white flowers; diminutive.

Barbados Cherry (*Malpighia glabra*): fine foliage; pink flowers.

Bottlebrush (*Callistemon citrinus*) 'Little John': dense, petite foliage; free branching; showy, red bottlebrush flowers.

Bougainvillea: 'Golden Glow', 'Louise Wathen' (orange to lilac), 'Magnifica' (purple), 'Mrs Butt' (fuschia), 'Pink Pixie', 'Snow White'

Flamboyant (*Delonix regia*): finely divided leaves, preferable to start this from seeds and to begin training early; deciduous.

Mile Tree (*Casuarina equisetifolia*): unique jointed 'leaves'; lovely bark.

Ming Aralia (*Polyscias fruticosa*): small plants with interesting, finely divided leaves.

Natal Plum (*Carissa macrocarpa*): dark-green foliage; white flowers; prized for the cascade effect.

Orange Jessamine (*Murraya exotica*): glossy green leaves; fragrant white blooms.

Pomegranate (*Punica granata*): glossy oval leaves; scarlet blooms.

West Indian Holly (*Malpighia coccigera*): prickly, glossy green leaves; pale pink flowers.

Yellow Rim (*Serrisa foetida*): evergreen, plain or variegated foliage; single or double white flowers.

Appendix II
Suggestions for Terrarium Planting

Dieffenbachia davidsei: bamboo-like in stature; reddish brown splashed stem circled white at joints; leaves, small, green with mahogany veining beneath; petioles winged and speckled; large terrarium; propagate from cuttings.

Dorstenia carnulosa: exotic succulent plant having small leaves, an interesting stem and curious 'blooms'; for a drier terrarium in bright light; propagate from seeds.

Ficus pumila: various cultivars of creeping figs, some with leaves variegated white or chartreuse, lobed or puckered; variegations develop best under cooler conditions; propagate from cuttings.

Fittonia (Nerve Plant): various silver or pink fishnet veins; creeping miniature plants needing high humidity; propagate from cuttings.

Neoregelia 'Fireball': dwarf, 10–15 cm (4–5 in) diameter rosette turns red when plant blooms; propagate from offsets.

Peperomia reptilis: creeping plant having tiny cupped, copper-coloured leaves about 1 cm long; propagate by cuttings.

Pilea semidentata: cute diminutive plant having mounds of pointed leaves topped with pinkish flowers; propagate by division.

Tillandsia bergeri: tiny grey-green rosettes of pointed leaves 2–5 cm (1–2 in) long; flowers magenta and yellow; propagate by offsets.

Appendix III
Variegated Foliage Suggestions

Herbaceous plants

Anthurium 'Powys Pride': deep pink spathes and splashed foliage.
Blue Ginger (*Dichorisandra thrysiflora variegata*): upright, stout succulent stems with silver-streaked, glossy, spirally-arranged foliage.
Canna ('Nirvana', 'Bangkok Yellow', 'King of Siam', 'Bengal Tiger'): tall plants; striped and/or mottled foliage; yellow/orange blooms.
Dwarf Variegated Shell Ginger (*Alpinia speciosa* (Zerumbet)): lovely gold and green, dwarf version of a popular garden plant.
Golden Water Zinnia (*Wedelia trilobata* 'Outenreath Gold'): three-lobed leaves splashed gold on green.
Ivory Stepladder Plant (*Costus dubius*): pot; light shade.
Lantana camara 'Greg Grant', 'Samantha': full sun; pots and tubs.
Pepper 'Thai Variegated': basket; sun.
Reed Stem Orchid (*Epidendrum radicans variegatum*): tub; sun.
Variegated Spanish Thyme (*Coleus amboinicus*): basket; sun.
Variegated Spider Lily (*Hymenocallis* 'Variegata'): tub; sun to semi-shade

Trees and shrubs

Bougainvillea
  'Royal Bengal Red': red bracts against variegated foliage.
  'Raspberry Ice': naturally low growing with bright pink bracts and ivory-edged leaves.
Chaste Tree (*Vitex agnus-castus variegata*): grey-green aromatic foliage variegated cream; fragrant lilac terminal inflorescence.
Hibiscus 'Carnival': remarkable miniature form of the variegated hedging hibiscus, *H. cooperi*. Splashed glossy foliage marked ivory and pink; flowers rose red; full sun; keep pruned to induce new growth and more flowers.
Natal Plum (*Carissa humphreyii variegata*): waxy, dark-green leaves edged white.
Turk's Cap Hibiscus (*Malvaviscus germanderii* 'Fiesta'): dwarf Turk's Cap hibiscus having striking leaf variegation and red flowers.

Appendix IV
Useful Resources on the World Wide Web

Bamboos

American Bamboo Society World Wide Web Page
http://www.bamboo.org/abs/index.shtml

Direct enquiries about the ABS to:
Michael Bartholomew,
Newsletter Editor
750 Krumkill Road, Albany,
NY 12203-5976, USA

Florida-Caribbean Chapter of ABS
http://www.bamboo.org/abs/FloridaCaribChapterInfo.html

Direct enquiries about the Florida-Caribbean Chapter to:
Elizabeth Haverfield,
President FCC-ABS
755 Tiziano Avenue, Coral Gables,
FL 33143-6263, USA

Bamboo Collectibles
http://www.earthworks.com/bamboo/index.html

Bonsai

Bonsai Societies of Florida
http://www.addimension.com/bonsai/bsf.html

Bonsai Clubs International
http://www.bonsai-bci.com/

Direct enquiries about Bonsai Clubs International to:
BCI Business Manager
PO Box 1176, Brookfield,
WI 53008-1176

The Bonsai Primer
http://www.wmin.ac.uk/~allen/main.html#Index

Comprehensive notes on bonsai culture

Bromeliads

Bromeliad-related Sites
http://www.selfin.org/bsst/links.htm

Photo album, mail order sources

Useful information about bromeliads
http://hammock.ifas.ufl.edu/txt/fairs/mg/10222.html

Container plant sources and resources

Garden Forum: Tropicals
http://www.gardenweb.com/forums/tropical/

A discussion group for those growing tropical plants indoors or outdoors

Appendix IV

Glasshouse Works
http://www.rareplants.com/pageone.html

Catalogue of interesting plant material including tropicals and succulents

Glasshouse Works
Church Street, PO Box 97,
Stewart, OH 45778-0097

Horticultural Digest
http://www.agrss.sheman.hawaii.edu/hort/digest/index.html

Hawaii Cooperative Extension Service, CTAHR, Department of Horticulture

Many useful articles on palm seed germination, pest control, orchids

Oglesby
http://www.oglesbytc.com

Wholesale source of Anthuriums, Spathiphyllums, Syngoniums Cultivars are illustrated in colour

Southern Perennials and Herbs
http://www.s-p-h.com/

98 Bridges Road, Tylertown, MS 39667-9338, USA

Nursery source of gingers, woody shrubs, trees and vines, books

In USA 1-800-774-0079

Stokes Tropicals
http://www.stokestropicals.com/tropical_treats.html

Stokes Tropicals,
PO Box 9868, New Iberia,
LA 70562-9868

E-mail:
<plants@stokestropicals.com>

Nursery source of bananas, gingers, frangipanis, heliconias, books

The Time–Life Plant Encyclopedia
http://cgi.pathfinder.com/@@wLVW6gQA6BBT1IPe/cgi-bin/VG/vg

Search by plant name, lighting, drainage, plant type, height, colour, and blooming season

The Ultimate Australian Gardening CD-ROM
http://gardeninfo.com/oz/2000.html

A demonstration site having many entries on indoor plants, cacti, succulents, orchids, ferns, palms, cycads

Plumerias (Frangipanis)

The Plumeria Society of America, Inc.
http://www.ruf.rice.edu/~miltonp/plumeria/PSAhome.html#start

Membership Committee
PO Box 22791 Houston,
TX 77227-2791

Seeds of all kinds

Exotic Seeds Newsgroup
http://www.aitcom.com/newsgroups/EXOTIC_SEEDS.htm

Discussion group for those interested in the germination of seeds

M.L. Farrar Pty. Ltd
http://www.peg.apc.org/~farrar/welcome.htm

86 Appendix IV

M.L. Farrar Pty. Ltd
International Seed Merchants
PO Box 1046, Bomaderry,
NSW 2541, Australia

Source of Australian native tree and shrub seed

Mesa Gardens
http://www.netlink.co.uk/users/mace/mesa/mesagard.html

Mesa Gardens
PO Box 72, Belem,
NM 87002, USA

E-mail: <cactus@swcp.com>

Source of cactus and succulent seeds

SBE'S Exotic, Tropical Plant Seed Catalogue
http://www.datasync.com/sbe/
(general catalogue)

http://www.datasync.com/sbe/cacti.html

Cactus and succulent seed listing

SBE, 3421 Bream Street, Gautier, MS 39553, USA

US Customers (Orders only)
1-800-336-2064

Overseas customers (voice and fax) 01-601-497-6544

World Seed On-Line Catalog
http://www.worldseed.com

E-mail: <Info@worldseed.com>

Worldwide Plant Seed Seedbank
http://www.seedman.com/

Appendix V
Plant Selection Guide

Botanical name	Height*	Lighting	Plant type	Uses	Grown for flowers	Grown for foliage
Achimenes	S	semi-shade	herbaceous	pot basket	✓	
Agave	M T	sun	herbaceous	pot tub		✓
Aglaonema	M	semi-shade	herbaceous	pot		✓
Aloe	S M T	sun	herbaceous	pot tub		✓
Anthurium	M	semi-shade	herbaceous	pot	✓	✓
Asparagus	M	sun semi-shade	herbaceous	pot basket		✓
Begonia	S M	semi-shade	herbaceous	pot basket terrarium	✓	✓

*Height at maturity when grown in a container
S, Short plant (under 30 cm)
M, Medium plant (30 cm–2 m)
T, Tall plant (over 2 m)

Botanical name	Height*	Lighting	Plant type	Uses	Grown for flowers	Grown for foliage
Beloperone	M	semi-shade	herbaceous	pot	✓	
Bidens	M	sun	herbaceous	basket	✓	
Bougainvillea	M T	sun	woody	pot basket tub	✓	
Bromeliads	S M T	sun semi-shade	herbaceous epiphyte or terrestrial	pot basket mounted	✓	✓
Brugsmansia (Datura)	M T	sun	herbaceous to woody	pot tub	✓	
Caladium	M	semi-shade	herbaceous	pot		✓
Carissa	S M	semi-shade	woody	pot bonsai		✓
Catharanthus	S M	sun	herbaceous	pot basket	✓	
Chlorophytum	M	semi-shade	herbaceous	basket		✓
Citrus	T	sun	woody	tub patio tree	✓	

Botanical name	Height*	Lighting	Plant type	Uses	Grown for flowers	Grown for foliage
Codiaeum	M T	sun semi-shade	woody	pot tub patio tree		✓
Coleus	S M	semi-shade sun	herbaceous	pot		✓
Crassula	S	sun	herbaceous	pot basket		✓
Cuphea	S	sun	woody	pot	✓	
Dieffenbachia	M	semi-shade	herbaceous	pot tub		✓
Dracaena	S M T	shade	woody	pot tub		✓
Duranta	M T	semi-shade sun	woody	tub	✓	
Euphorbia	S M	sun	herbaceous	pot		✓
Ficus	S M T	sun	woody	pot terrarium		✓
Fittonia	S	semi-shade	herbaceous	terrarium		✓

Botanical name	Height*	Lighting	Plant type	Uses	Grown for flowers	Grown for foliage
Hibiscus	M T	sun	woody	pot tub patio tree	✓	
Hippeastrum	M	sun semi-shade	herbaceous	pot	✓	
Howea	M T	semi-shade shade	palm	pot		✓
Impatiens	S M	semi-shade sun	herbaceous	pot basket	✓	
Jasminium	M T	sun	woody vine	pot basket trellis	✓	
Lagerstroemia	M T	sun	woody	pot tub bonsai	✓	
Lantana	S M	sun	woody	pot basket	✓	
Maranta	S M	semi-shade	herbaceous	pot		✓
Orchids	S M	semi-shade	herbaceous	pot basket mounted	✓	

Botanical name	Height*	Lighting	Plant type	Uses	Grown for flowers	Grown for foliage
Peperomia	S M	semi-shade shade	herbaceous	pot basket		✓
Pilea	S	semi-shade shade	herbaceous	terrarium		✓
Platycerium	M	semi-shade	herbaceous fern	mounted		✓
Plumeria	M T	sun	woody	tub	✓	
Polyscias (Aralia)	M	sun semi-shade	woody	pot tub		✓
Saintpaulia	S	semi-shade	herbaceous	pot	✓	
Sinningia	S	semi-shade	herbaceous	pot terrarium	✓	
Verbena	S	sun	herbaceous	pot basket	✓	
Zinnia	S M	sun	herbaceous annual	pot basket	✓	

* Height at maturity when grown in a container
S, Short plant (under 30 cm)
M, Medium plant (30 cm–2 m)
T, Tall plant (over 2 m)

Appendix VI
Plant and Seed Sources*

Container plant sources

Glasshouse Works

Church Sreet, PO Box 97,
Stewart, OH 45778-0097,
USA

Catalogue of interesting plant material including tropicals and succulents

Hamlyn Orchids Limited
Claude W. Hamilton and Family
31 King's House Avenue,
Kingston, Jamaica, WI
Tel: 1-876-927-6713
Fax: 1-876-978-6888
E-mail:<hamlyn@infochan.com>

Orchid plants, seedlings and flasks, Broughtonia hybrids, etc.

Rapis Gardens
PO Box 287, Gregory
TX 78359, USA

Nursery specializing in Lady Palms (Rapis excelsa), Sago Palms (Cycas revoluta) and Ming Aralias (Polycias)

Southern Perennials and Herbs
98 Bridges Road, Tylertown,
MS 39667-9338, USA

Nursery source of gingers, woody shrubs, trees and vines, books

Stokes Tropicals
PO Box 9868, New Iberia,
LA 70562-9868

Nursery source of bananas, frangipanis, gingers, heliconias, books

Seeds of all kinds

M.L. Farrar Pty. Ltd
International Seed Merchants
PO Box 1046, Bomaderry,
NSW 2541, Australia

Source of Australian native tree and shrub seed

Mesa Gardens
PO Box 72, Belem,
NM 87002, USA

Source of cactus and succulent seeds

---

* No guarantee of quality or satisfaction is implied

Geo. W. Park Seed Co., Inc.
1 Parkton Avenue,
Greenwood,
SC 29647-0001, USA

Source of flower and vegetable seeds

SBE'S Exotic, Tropical Plant Seed Catalogue
SBE
3421 Bream Street, Gautier,
MS 39553 USA

Palm, cactus, succulents and many other plant types

Glossary

Air layering (marcottage)   A method of plant propagation: a wounded stem is induced to produce roots from a node by wrapping it with damp moss enclosed in an impervious layer such as a plastic wrap.

Annual   A plant that grows to produce flowers, seeds, then dies all in one growing season.

Balanced fertilizer   A fertilizer that contains all major plant nutrients (nitrogen, phosphorus and potassium) and all of the minor nutrients as well.

Cephalium   A perennial flowering structure which grows gradually with a plant such as the Turk's Cap Cactus, Melocactus.

Chelated iron (sequestered iron)   A product where iron and sometimes other reactive minerals are chemically bound to remain soluble and available to plants.

Chlorosis   Yellowed foliage, particularly where the veins remain green. A situation caused by mineral deficiency or imbalance, often exacerbated by inappropriate soil pH.

Clone   A unique individual that may be propagated only by vegetative means.

Coconut cloth   The fibrous remnant of Coconut Palm leaf bases resembling canvas or burlap cloth.

Compost   Product prepared from decomposing waste plant material.

Cultivar   A selected plant variety chosen for particular superior qualities such as flower colour and size. Cultivars may only be propagated by cuttings, grafts, marcots or tissue culture.

Deciduous   A plant that drops its leaves in response to changing seasons or stress.

Division   Propagation method whereby a plant is divided into two or more rooted parts.

Dormancy   Certain plants periodically cease active growth and sometimes also drop their leaves. The onset of dormancy often coincides with the dry season.

Epiphyte   A plant that lives rooted on the bark of trees and not rooted in soil.

Fernery   A shaded place where ferns are cultivated.

Fertilizer   A source of plant mineral nutrients that may be added to soil or sprayed on plants to correct possible deficiencies.

Fungicide A product used to control plant diseases caused by fungi (*sing*. fungus).
Germination The process by which a seed becomes a plant.
Grafting A method of vegetative propagation: a piece of the desirable plant is united with a more vigorous rootstock.
Hormone rooting powder A product containing one or more plant hormones (auxins) in a powder form which when applied to cuttings may accelerate the rooting process.
Host plant A plant attacked and weakened by bacteria, fungus or viruses. A plant providing physical support to epiphytes.
Hybrid A cross between two species in an attempt to obtain an improved plant. Seeds of hybrid plants will not necessarily wholly resemble the seed parent.
Infestation A condition when a plant is attacked by pests.
Keiki Offsets produced by orchids.
Latex A milky white or coloured fluid product of certain plants such as Poinsettia.
Leaching The action of water to dissolve minerals and carry them away.
Marcot (air layer) A procedure by which roots are induced to form along a stem without severing the part from the parent plant.
Micronutrient Plant nutrients including magnesium, manganese and zinc that are essential to plant health but required only in small quantities.
Mites (Spider Mites) Tiny plant pests related to spiders that attack leaves and suck plant juices.
Mulch A layer of organic matter that is applied to soil to protect the surface from erosion and to conserve moisture.
Nematicide A product used to kill nematodes.
Nematode (Eelworm) Tiny plant pests found mainly in soil that attack plant roots leading to a reduction in the ability to absorb water and nutrients.
Node Point along a stem where buds, shoots and flowers originate.
Offset A shoot arising from the base of a plant or occasionally from a stem (as in orchids), or from an inflorescence (as in Alpinia).
Patio tree A shrub or tree trained to have an extraordinarily long stem without branching except at the top where this is encouraged by pinching and pruning.
Perennial A plant that, once mature, maintains a yearly reproductive cycle.
Perlite™ A white, porous pumice product that can be used in combination with other materials to make a porous rooting medium.
Pesticide A product used to kill plant pests including insects, mites, slugs and weeds.
Petiole The part of a leaf that extends from the flattened blade to the stem.
pH A symbol used to describe the relative acidity or alkalinity of a substance such as soil.

Pinch (pinch back) A term used to describe the removal of growing points to induce bushy growth.
Porosity A term that refers to the spaces between soil particles which allow passage of air and water.
Propagation Methods by which plants are multiplied including by seed, by cuttings, by grafting or by division.
Pruning The process by which woody plants are trained by the removal of excess branches or roots.
Pseudobulb Annual swollen shoots of certain orchids such as *Cattleya*.
Pseudostem Bananas and similar plants have a 'stem' composed of many layers of leaf bases. The true stem is at the ground level.
Resistance The natural means by which some plants ward off pests and diseases.
Rhizome A prostrate underground stem.
Seed A plant reproductive unit.
Seedling A young plant before it has bloomed for the first time.
Slow-release fertilizer A product formulated to release mineral nutrients slowly over several months.
Spathe A protective and sometimes colourful leaf associated with the flowers of aroid plants.
Species A group of closely related plants. Plants raised from seed of a species will resemble that species.
Standard (*see* **Patio tree**)
Tetraploid (*4n*) Plants having four sets of chromosomes in place of the usual two sets (*2n*). Tetraploid cultivars often have larger and more substantial flowers and foliage.
Variegation Variable leaf markings usually seen as stripes or blotches of white on green but also occurring in shades of green, gold and pink.
Variety A horticulturally desirable plant often bearing a varietal name.
Vermiculite An expanded mica product sometimes used as a soil amendment or as a soil additive to improve moisture-holding capacity and porosity.
Viviparous Plants which give rise to plantlets on their leaves as in certain waterlilies and ferns.
Wicking A procedure by which a length of candle wick is placed in a container and permitted to protrude into the saucer to absorb water.

Bibliography

BANNOCHIE, I. and LIGHT, M., *Gardening in the Caribbean*, Macmillan Publishers Ltd, Basingstoke, England (1993)
BEERS, L. and HOWIE, J., *Growing Hibiscus*, 3rd edn, Kangaroo Press (1996), ISBN 0-86417-506-x
BERRY, F. and KRESS, W.J., *Heliconia: An Identification Guide*, Smithsonian Institution Press, Washington and London (1991)
CHAPMAN, T.S., *Ornamental Gingers: A Guide to Selection and Cultivation*, 2nd edn, T.S. Chapman, St Gabriel, Louisiana, LA 70776-5602, USA (1995)
EGGENBERGER, R.M. and EGGENBERGER, M.H., *Handbook of Plumeria Culture*, 3rd edn, Tropical Plant Specialists (1994), ISBN 0-9643224-0-4
GREENOAK, F., *Water Features for Small Gardens*, Conran Octopus (1996)
JONES, D.L., *Palms Throughout the World*, Smithsonian Institution Press (1995)
LIGHT, M., *Growing Orchids in the Caribbean*, Macmillan Publishers Ltd, Basingstoke, England (1995)
OGDEN, S., *Garden Bulbs for the South*, Taylor (1996)
ROWLEY, G., *The Illustrated Encyclopedia of Succulents*, Salamander Books Ltd, London, England (1978)
SEABORN, B., *Bromeliads: Tropical Air Plants*, Gick Publishing, Inc., Laguna Hills, California, USA (1976)
SLOCUM, P.D., ROBINSON, P. and PERRY, F., *Water Gardening – Water Lilies and Lotuses*, Timber Press, USA (1996)
VANDERPLANK, J., *Passion Flowers*, Cassel (1996)

Index of Plant Names

Acalypha wilkesiana (Match-me-Not)   73
Achimenes (Gesneriad)   54, 87
Achimenes antirrhina (Achimenes)   54, 87
Achimenes erecta (Achimenes)   54, 87
Adiantum (Maidenhair Fern)   52, 53
Aechmea blumenavil (Bromeliad)   35
Aechmea distichantha (Bromeliad)   35
Aechmea fasciata (Bromeliad)   61
Aechmea pineliana (Bromeliad)   35
Aechynanthus lobbianus (Lipstick Plant)   56
Agapanthus (Lily of the Nile)   9, 47
Aglaonema (Chinese Evergreen)   17, 87
Alocasia cuprea (Aroid)   47
Aloe aristata (Aloe)   51
Aloe variegata (Aloe)   51
Alpinia speciosa (Dwarf Variegated Shell Ginger)   63
Alsobia dianthiflora (Episcia)   55
Alsobia punctata (Episcia)   55
Alsophila australis (Australian Tree Fern)   53
Alternathera ficoidea (Calico Plant)   59, 81
Alternathera polygonoides (Water Amaranth)   80
Amaranthus caudatus (Love Lies Bleeding)   60
Amazon Lily (*Eucharis grandiflora*)   45

Ananas (Pineapple, Bromeliad)   61
Angel's Trumpet (*Brugsmansia*; *Datura*)   57, 88
Anthurium   63, 83, 87
Arabian Jasmine (*Jasminium sambac*)   73
Arrowroot (*Canna concinna*)   79
Ascocenda (Orchid)   66
Asparagus   81
Asparagus densiflorus (Foxtail Asparagus, Sprenger Asparagus)   25, 63, 64
Asparagus Fern (Asparagus)   25, 63, 64
Asplenium (Bird's Nest Fern)   52
Asplenium bulbiferum (Mother Fern)   53
Astrophytum (Bishop's Cap Cactus)   49
Australian Tree Fern (*Alsophila australis*; *Sphaeropteris cooperi*)   53
Averrhoa carambola (Star Fruit)   75

Balsam (*Impatiens balsamifera*)   61
Banana (*Musa*)   36, 70, 75
Basil (*Ocimum*)   39, 40, Pl. 3.1
Bauhinia galpinii (Nasturtium Bauhinia)   69
Bauhinia purpurea (Orchid Tree)   69
Bauhinia variegata (Orchid Tree)   69
Beaucarnia (Pony Tail Tree)   73
Bee Orchid (*Oncidium*)   65
Begonia rex (Rex Begonia)   26
Bidens   36, 57, 88, Pl. 1.4

Index of Plant Names 99

Billbergia (Bromeliad) Pl. 11.2
Bird Catcher Tree (*Pisonia brunoniana*) 70, Pl. 8.3
Bird's Nest Fern (*Asplenium*) 52
Bishop's Cap Cactus (*Astrophytum*) 49
Blood Banana (*Musa zebrina*) 75
Blue Ginger (*Dichorisandra thrysiflora*) 63, 83
Blue Potato Shrub (*Solanum rantonnettii*) 73
Blue Trumpet Vine (*Thunbergia grandiflora*) 76
Boston Fern (*Nephrolepis* spp., *N. cordifolia*) 25, 52
Bottle Palm (*Hyophorbe lagenicaulis*) 73
Bougainvillea 10, 42, 73, 77, 81, 88
Brassavola nodosa (Lady-of-the-Night) 65
Brazilian Sky Flower (*Duranta repens*) 71, 74
Breadfruit Fern (*Polypodium*) 52, Pl. 5.3
Bromeliad (*Aechmea, Ananas, Billbergia, Guzmania, Neoregelia, Tillandsia*) 25, 35, 61, 82, 88, Pl. 1.3, 11.1, 11.2
Broughtonia (Orchid) 66
Browallia 62
Brugmansia (Angel's Trumpet) 57, 88, Pl. 5.1
Bush Convolvulus (*Convolvulus*) 58
Bush lantana (*Lantana camara*) 74, 83

Caesalpinia pulcherrima (Pride of Barbados) 74
Caladium 9, 45, 88
Calathea fasciata (Calathea) 63
Calathea majestica (Calathea) 63
Calathea picturata (Calathea) 63
Calathea roseo-picta (Calathea) 63
Calico Plant (*Alternathera ficoidea*) 59
Calliandra surinamensis (Surinam Powder Puff) 74
Calonyction (Moonflower) 76
Canariensis (*Galphimia gracilis*) Pl. 3.2

Canna 46, 49, 83, Pl. 1.1
Canna concinna (Arrowroot) 79
Cardboard Palm (*Zamia*) 67
Carissa 88
Carissa grandiflora (*macrocarpa*) (Carissa) 42, 81
Caryota mitis (Clustered Fishtail Palm) 68
Catharanthus roseus (Periwinkle) 36, 60, 88
Cattleya skinneri (Orchid) 35, 65
Chamaedorea (Reed Palm) 17, 67, 68
Chamaedorea seifrizii (Reed Palm) 68
Chaste Tree (*Vitex agnus-castus*) 70
Chrysalidocarpus lutescens (Golden Palm) 69
Cigar Plant (*Cuphea micropetala*) 60
Citrus (Orange, Lemon, Lime, Grapefruit, Pommelo) 14, 36, 70, 75, 88, Pl. 2.1
Cleome (Spider Flower) 58
Clockvine (*Thunbergia alata*) 76
Clustered Fishtail Palm (*Caryota mitis*) 68
Codiaeum (Croton) 73, 89
Coleus 62, 63, 89, Pl. 3.2
Coleus amboinicus (Variegated Spanish Thyme) 39, 60, Pl. 3.3
Coleus aromaticus (Spanish Thyme) 60
Colocasia antiquorum illustris (Aroid) 47
Columnea (Gesneriad) 56, Pl. 4.3
Convolvulus (Bush Convolvulus) 58
Coontie (*Zamia floradana*) 67
Cosmos 60
Costus dubius (Ivory Stepladder Plant) 64, 83
Crape Myrtle (*Lagerstroemia*) 71, 73
Crassula (Succulent) 51, 84, Pl. 6.2
Crimson Passionflower (*Passiflora vitifolia*) 77
Crinum 45, Pl. 9.3
Crossandra 60
Croton (*Codiaeum*) 73

100 Index of Plant Names

Crown-of-Thorns (*Euphorbia milii*) Pl. 6.1
Cryptanthus (Bromeliad) 61
Cuban Oregano (*Coleus amboinicus*) 39
Cuphea hyssopifolia (Mexican Heather) 72, 89, Pl. 8.4
Cuphea ignea (Firecracker Plant) 60
Cuphea micropetala (Cigar Plant) 60
Cycad (*Cycas*; *Encephalartos*; *Zamia*) 66, 68, Pl. 7.4
Cyperus haspans (Dwarf Umbrella Plant) 12, 78

Davalia (Rabbit's Foot Fern) 52, 58
Dendrobium (orchid) 26
Dichorisandra thrysiflora (Blue Ginger) 63, 83
Dieffenbachia (Dumb Cane) 63, 82, 89, Pl. 1.2
Dieffenbachia amoena (Dumb Cane) 63
Dominican Oregano (*Lippa micromeris*) 39
Doritaenopsis (Moth Orchid) 65, 66
Dracaena 73, 89, Pl. 8.1
Dracaena marginata (Dracaena) 73
Draceana terminalis (Dracaena) 74
Dumb Cane (*Dieffenbachia*) 63
Duranta repens (Golden Dewdrop, Brazilian Sky Flower) 71, 74, 89
Dwarf Poinciana (*Caesalpinia pulcherrima*) 74
Dwarf Shrimp Plant (*Justicia brandegeanna*) 63
Dwarf Umbrella Plant (*Cyperus haspans*) 78
Dwarf Variegated Shell Ginger (*Alpinia speciosa* (Zerumbet)) 63, 83

Earth Star (*Cryptanthus*) 61
Echeveria (Succulent) 34
Eichornia (Water Hyacinth) 78
Eleocharis dulcis (Variegated Chinese Water Chestnut) 79
Elephant Ears (*Alocasia*; *Colocasia*; *Xanthosoma*) 46

Encephalartos ferox (Cycad) 68
Encephalartos munchii (Cycad) 68, Pl. 7.4
Epidendrum (Orchid) 26, 66
Epidendrum radicans variegatum (Orchid) 66, 83
Episcia (Gesneriad) 55, Pl. 4.1
Erythrina humeana (Raja Coral Tree) 74
Espostoa (Old Man of the Andes Cactus) 49
Eucharis grandiflora (Amazon Lily, Eucharis Lily) 45
Eucharis Lily (*Eucharis grandiflora*) 45
Euphorbia milii (Crown-of-Thorns) 51, 89
Euphorbia obesa (Euphorbia) 51

Feijoa sellowiana (Pineapple Guava) 75
Ficus benjamina (Weeping Fig) 42, 74, 89
Ficus carica (Edible Fig) 75
Fig (*Ficus carica*) 75
Fiji Fan Palm (*Pritchardia pacifica*) 68
Firecracker Plant (*Cuphea ignea*) 60
Fishtail Palm (*Caryota mitis*) 68
Fittonia 63, 82, 89
Four O'Clock (*Mirabilis*) 60
Foxtail Asparagus (*Asparagus densiflorus*) 63
Frangipani (*Plumeria*) 28, 71, 74

Galphimia gracilis (Canariensis) Pl. 3.2
Gerbera (Transvaal Daisy) 16, 62
Giant Moth Ginger (*Hedychium hasseltii*) 63
Globe Amaranth (*Gomphrena*) 60
Gloriosa Lily (*Gloriosa*) 9, Figure 3a, c, d
Glory Bush (*Tibouchina urvilleana*) 74
Gloxinia perennis (Gesneriad) 55
Golden Dewdrop (*Duranta repens*) 71, 74
Golden Palm (*Chrysalidocarpus lutescens*) 69

Index of Plant Names 101

Golden Pothos (*Scindapsus aureus*) 17
Golden Water Zinnia (*Wedelia trilobata*) 60, 83
Gomphrena (Globe Amaranth) 60
Grapefruit (*Citrus*) 14, 36, 70, 75, 88
Graptopetalum (Succulent) 26
Ground Orchid (Spathoglottis) 2
Guzmania (Bromeliad) 64

Hedychium hasseltii (Giant Moth Ginger) 63
Hemigraphis 'Exotica' (Variegated Waffle Plant) 79
Hibiscus 72, 90
Howea fosteriana (Kentia Palm) 68, 90
Hydrocleys nymphoides (Water Poppy) 80
Hymenocallis (Spider Lily) 48

Impatiens 61, 64, 90, Pl. 3.4
Impatiens balsamifera (Balsam) 61, 64
Ipomoea (Morning Glory, Dwarf Morning Glory) 58
Ivory Stepladder Plant (*Costus dubius*) 64, 83
Ixora 74

Jasminium grandiflorum (Spanish Jasmine) 77
Jasminium sambac (Arabian Jasmine) 73
Jasminium volubile 'Mediopicta' 77
Justicia brandegeeana (Dwarf Shrimp Plant) 63

Kentia Palm (*Howea fosteriana*) 68

Lady-of-the-Night (*Brassavola nodosa*) 65
Lady Palm (*Rhapis excelsa*) 66, 68
Lagerstroemia indica (Crape Myrtle, Queen-of-the-Flowers) 42, 71, 73, 90
Lantana (Sage) 72, 74, 90
Lantana camara (Sage, Bush Lantana) 74, 83

Lantana sellowiana (Sage, Trailing Lantana) Pl. 9.1
Licuala grandis (Round Leaf Palm) 69
Lily of the Nile (*Agapanthus*) 47
Lime (*Citrus*) 14, 36, 70, 75, 88
Lippa micromera (Dominican Oregano) 39
Lipstick Plant (*Aechyanthus*) 56
Lotus (*Nelumbo*) 12, 78, Pl. 10.2
Love Lies Bleeding (*Amaranthus caudatus*) 60
Ludwigia sidioides (Mosaic Plant) 79

Maidenhair Fern (*Adiantum*) 52
Malpighia coccigera (West Indian Holly) 42, 81
Mammillaria compressa (Cactus) 50
Mammillaria elegans (Cactus) 50
Mammillaria erythrosperma (Cactus) 50
Mammillaria uncinata (Cactus) 50
Mammillaria zuccariniana (Cactus) 50
Mandevilla 77
Mandevilla sanderi (Mandevilla) 77
Maranta leuconeura (Prayer Plant) 64, 90
Marigold (*Tagetes*) 58
Marjoram 39
Melampodium 60
Melocactus (Cactus) 50
Mexican Heather (*Cuphea hyssopifolia*) 72
Mexican Tarragon (*Tagetes lucida*) 39
Ming Aralia (*Polyscias fruticosa*) 74, 81
Mirabilis (Four O'Clock) 60
Moonflower (*Calonyction*) 76
Morning Glory (*Convolvulus; Ipomoea*) 58
Mosaic Plant (*Ludwigia sidioides*) 79
Mother Fern (*Asplenium bulbiferum*) 53
Moth Orchid (*Phalaenopsis*) 65, 66
Mountain Ebony (*Bauhinia purpurea*) 69

Musa ornata (Banana)   70, 75
Musa velutina (Banana)   70, 75, Pl. 2.3
Musa zebrina (Banana)   70, 75

Narcissus tazetta (Paperwhite Narcissus)   47
Nasturtium Bauhinia (*Bauhinia galpinii*)   69
Nelumbo (Lotus)   12, 78
Neoregelia (Bromeliad)   35, 61, Pl. 1.3
Nephrolepis cordifolia (Boston Fern)   52
Nerium oleander (Oleander)   72
Nicotiana   58
Nymphaea (Waterlily)   12, 79
Nymphoides geminata (Yellow Snowflake)   78
Nymphoides indica (White Snowflake)   78

Ocimum (Basil)   39
Old Man of the Andes Cactus (*Espostoa*)   49
Oleander (*Nerium oleander*)   72
Oncidium ampliatum (Bee Orchid)   65
Orchid (*Ascocenda; Broughtonia; Cattleya; Epidendrum; Oncidium; Vanda*)   64, 65, 90, Pl. 7.1, 7.2, 7.3
Orchid Tree (*Bauhinia purpurea*)   69

Palm   66
Paperwhite Narcissus (*Narcissus tazetta*)   47
Paphiopedilum (Lady's-slipper, Orchid)   65
Papyrus (*Cyperus*)   12
Parodia (Cactus)   50, Pl. 6.4
Partridge-breasted Aloe (*Aloe variegata*)   51
Passiflora cuspidifolia (Watermelon Leaf Passionflower)   77
Passiflora vitifolia (Crimson Passionflower)   77
Peperomia   7, 91, Figure 2b, c, d
Pepper (*Solanum*)   60, 83
Periwinkle (*Catharanthus roseus*)   36, 60
Petunia   36, 59, Pl. 1.4

Phalaenopsis (Orchid)   26, 65, 66
Pineapple Guava (*Feijoa sellowiana*)   75
Pisonia brunoniana (Bird Catcher Tree)   70
Pistia (Water Lettuce)   78
Platycerium bifurcatum (Staghorn Fern)   52, 53, 91
Plumeria (Frangipani)   28, 71, 74, 91
Polianthes (Tuberose)   48
Polypodium (Breadfruit Fern)   52
Polyscias fruticosa (Ming Aralia)   74, 81, 91
Pomegranate (*Punica*)   81, Pl. 9.2
Pommelo (*Citrus*)   14, 36, 70, 75
Pony Tail Tree (*Beaucarnia*)   73
Portulaca   18, 34, 60
Prayer Plant (*Maranta leuconeura*)   64
Pride of Barbados (*Caesalpinia pulcherrima*)   74
Pritchardia pacifica (Fiji Fan Palm)   68
Punica (Pomegranate)   81

Queen of Flowers (*Lagerstroemia*)   71

Rabbit's-Foot Fern (*Davalia*)   52, 53
Rhapis excelsa (Lady Palm)   68
Raja Coral Tree (*Erythrina*)   74
Reed Palm (*Chamaedorea*)   17, 66
Reed Stem Orchid (*Epidendrum*)   66
Rex Begonia (*Begonia rex*)   26
Rhipsalis (Cactus)   51, Pl. 6.3
Rosemary   40, 42, Figure 11a–d
Round Leaf Palm (*Licuala grandis*)   69

Sage (*Lantana camara, L. sellowiana*)   74, 83, Pl. 9.1
Saintpaulia (African Violet)   26, 54, 91
Scindapsus aureus (Golden Pothos)   17
Sentry Palm (*Howea fosteriana*)   68
Serissa foetida (Yellow-rim)   42, 81
Sinningia cardinalis (Gesneriad)   56, 91

Index of Plant Names 103

Solanum rantonnettii (Blue Potato Shrub) 73
Spanish Jasmine (*Jasminium grandiflorum*) 77
Spanish Thyme (*Coleus aromaticus*) 69, Pl. 3.3
Spathoglottis (Ground Orchid) 2
Sphaeropteris cooperi (Australian Tree Fern) 53
Spider Flower (*Cleome*) 58
Spider Lily (*Hymenocallis*) 48
Sprenger Asparagus (*Asparagus densiflorus*) 64
Staghorn Fern (*Platycerium bifurcatum*) 52, 53, Pl. 5.2
Star Fruit (*Averrhoa carambola*) 75, Pl. 2.4
Streptocarpella saxorum 56, Pl. 4.2
Surinam Powder Puff (*Calliandra surinamensis*) 74
Syngonium podophyllum 64

Tagetes (Marigold) 36, 58
Tagetes lucida (Mexican Tarragon) 39
Tangelo (*Citrus*) 14, 36, 70, 75, 88
Tangerine (*Citrus*) 14, 36, 70, 75, 88
Thunbergia alata (Clockvine) 76
Thunbergia grandiflora (Blue Trumpet Vine) 76
Tibouchina urvilleana (Glory Bush) 74
Torenia flava (Torenia) 68
Torenia fournieri (Wishbone Flower) 62
Trailing Lantana (*Lantana sellowiana* Pl. 9.1
Transvaal Daisy (*Gerbera*) 15, 62
Tuberose (*Polianthes*) 2, 9, 48

Umbrella Sedge (*Cyperus haspans*) 12, 78

Vanda (Orchid) 26, 66
Variegated Australian Jasmine (*Jasminium volubile* 'Mediopicta') 77
Variegated Chinese Water Chestnut (*Eleocharis dulcis* 'Variegata') 79

Variegated Spanish Thyme (*Coleus amboinicus*) 60, 83
Variegated Waffle Plant (*Hemigraphis*) 79
Verbena 36, 59, 91
Victoria amazonica (Water Platter) 77
Vitex agnus-castus (Chaste Tree) 70
Vriesea (Bromeliad) 64

Water Amaranth (*Alternathera polygonoides*) 80
Water Canna (*Canna*) 77
Water Hyacinth (*Eichornia*) 11, 78, Pl. 10.4
Water Lettuce (*Pistia*) 11, 26, 78
Waterlily (*Nymphaea*) 12, 26, 79, Pl. 10.1
Watermelon Leaf Passionflower (*Passiflora cuspidifolia*) 77
Water Platter (*Victoria amazonica*) 77
Water Poppy (*Hydrocleys nymphoides*) 80
Wedelia trilobata (Wedelia, Golden Water Zinnia) 60, 83
Weeping Fig Tree (*Ficus benjamina*) 74
West Indian Holly (*Malpighia coccigera*) 42, 81
White Snowflake (*Nymphoides indica*) 78, Pl. 10.3

Xanthosoma saggitifolia (Aroid) 47

Yellow-rim (*Serissa foetida*) 42, 81
Yellow Snowflake (*Nymphoides geminata*) 78

Zamia floradana (Coontie) 67
Zamia furfuracea (Cardboard Palm) 67
Zamia pumila (Cardboard Palm) 67
Zephyranthes (Zephyr Lily) 48
Zephyr Lily (*Zephyranthes*) 48
Zinnia (*Zinnia angustifolia*) 36, 59, 91, Pl. 5.4
Zinnia angustifolia (Zinnia) 36, 59, 91, Pl. 5.4

General Index

Air-conditioning 15
Annuals 6, 56

Baskets 2, 6, 8, 31
Bonsai 6, 40, 43, 81, Pl. 11.3
Bottle gardens 38, 39
Bromeliad tree 35
Bulbs 6, 45

Cacti 6, 13, 24, 49
Chlorosis 14, 36
Choosing containers 23, 31, 42
Choosing plants 32
Climbers 76
Colour 34, 35
Compost 42
Cuttings 25, 26, 27

Diseases 20, 21, 22, 67
Division 24
Drought 32

Feeding plants 14
Fertilizer 12, 14, 36
Fruit 36, 75

Germination 29, 30
Growing bags 23, 36, 37, 39

Herbs 39, 40

Lighting 15, 18

Marcotting 28
Mealy bugs 20

Nematodes 19, 24

Over-watering 21

Palms 6, 14, 66, 69
Patio tree 37
Perennials 6, 56
Pests 19, 20, 21

Pinching 43
Pools 10, 11, 12, 77
Potting mixtures 6
Pots 2, 8
Propagation 24, 25, 29
Pruning 19, 28, 42, 43

Root bound 18
Root mealy bugs 20
Root pruning 19, 40, 41, 42
Roots 19

Salt tolerance 32, 67, 72
Seeds 28, 29
Shade 32, 61
Shrubs 6, 14, 27, 28, 69
Soil 3, 4, 12
Soil, heat treatment 3, 4
Soil-less mix 4
Spider mites 20
Succulent plants 6, 34
Supporting plants 38, 76
Standard tree 37, 38

Temperature 37
Terrariums 6, 12, 13, 14, 38
Tip burn 18, 21
Tools for terrariums 39
Training plants 40, 42, Pl. 11.3
Trees 6, 14, 27, 69, 74
Trellis 76
Tubers 45

Vegetables 23, 37

Watering 15, 39, Pl. 11.4
Water plants 6, 11, 12, 14, 26, 43, 77
Wicking 15
Wilting 21
Wind 2, 32